Can We Talk?

Letters & Poems to Reclaim a Bolder You

By

Lolita E. Walker

First Printing: 2022
ISBN: 978-1-7327928-2-1
Library of Congress Control Number: 2022901561

Published by Lolita E. Walker / Walker & Walker Enterprises, LLC.
16405 Livingston Road, #804
Accokeek, MD. 20607
https://www.lolitawalker.com

Previous Works: The Intersection of You & Change
Copyright © 2018 by Lolita E. Walker

Ordering Information:
Special discounts are available on quantity purchases by corporations, associations, educators, and the general public.

For details, contact the publisher at the above listed address.
U.S. trade bookstores and wholesalers: Please contact Walker & Walker Enterprises, LLC.
Tel: (443) 353-9121 or email info@lolitawalker.com

WALKER & WALKER
ENTERPRISES

2022

Dear Reader,
Can we talk?

THIS BOOK IS FOR YOU!
I welcome you to lean in and take a seat,
as I blanket my words and energy around you.

Few will take the challenge
of accepting this invited pause, for the cause -being you.

This book will uproot feelings and incite you to explore;
it will dig deep to uncover what may be something more,
hidden within you - within me.
Are you ready to experience your endless possibilities?

If you've ever felt vulnerable or forgotten,
experienced joy, triumph or pain;
if you've stumbled through heartbreak,
lost a loved one or felt shame,
these letters and poems create forums to shift you
and lift you – higher.

This is not about me and my story,
but to help you live in your glory,
to expand your mind, as you dare to find what may be buried inside.
What if you chose to release the guard, the armor, and the shield?
What If you chose to carry the white flag and let go, to now build?

This book will empower you - and your inner critic too.

Dear Reader,
Can we talk?

This is to you, from me.
I love you,

Lolita

THE DEDICATION

This book is dedicated to my maternal grandmother, Ms. Emma Beatrice Evans.

I am so blessed and excited for the opportunity to speak directly to her in this moment.

Dear Grandma Bea,

My hope is that these carefully crafted letters and poems help you to combat the sometimes, negative internal chatter that dares to creep into your mind.

I pray that my words have the power to meet you where you are, acknowledge and comfort you, then cover you when and how you need. I pray that they help to overtake any beliefs that may limit the greatness of who God has created you to be. May those beliefs flood every inch of you, with strengthened confidence and worth, increased self-love and a multitude of great memories that will continuously motivate and encourage you to live your best years as your most "be free."

At the seasoned age of 91 years young, you remain a blessing to me and all of those you surround. Grandma Bea, I have promised you this book for almost one year. Today, it is here for you to have and to hold for the rest of the days of your life.

Dear Grandma Bea,
This is to you, from me,
I love you.

Your granddaughter,
Lolita

THE CONTENTS

THE FOREWORD

By Damon Jones, Corporate Activist at the intersection of purpose, passion and the pursuit of what is right; Chief Communications Officer of The Procter & Gamble Company

One of the few rays of light created in the shadow of the pandemic is the time and space to take stock of what really matters. The question then naturally becomes 'what are we going to do about it?'

Shifting to the life we want to live requires a bold first step. That powerful first step is then followed by a journey of discovery and reflection, but thankfully one that you don't have to take alone. With the pages now in your possession, you have both a path and a partner.

Art unlocks human potential and comes in many forms. Great artists have the innate ability to connect our hearts and our minds and then motivate our hands to take action. They create awareness and spark creativity, then infuse into us new perspectives and the power of possibility. They connect our emotions and unlock our capabilities in unimaginable ways. Lolita beautifully demonstrates this artistry. Her colorful palette of letters and poems invite us to join her for an experience that will penetrate our minds and lift our spirits.

This is not "Self-Help 101." It is a unique resource that leads us to become more in-touch with our own greatness. It edges us toward progress and serves as a partner on our journey, walking side-by-side with us, not step-by-step before us, on what can feel like, a generic, prescriptive path to someone else's dreams.

Along the journey of self-discovery, we can find ourselves stuck and unsure of where to go. *"Can We Talk?"* deliberately shifts our mindsets to live the life we want and deserve to lead. Whether forging a new relationship, leaving one that no longer suits us, pouring into a passion, or experiencing an unplanned transition, Lolita's words lead us from being consumed with our right now, unable to see what is ahead, to more deeply acknowledging, then connecting to the emotions that are often difficult to express. They unlock doors to help us become the best version of ourselves.

The beauty of this compilation is that you will experience it in a way that is uniquely yours. Not designed to be read cover to cover or followed step-by-step, it is curated to connect you with what will serve you in your moment. It invites progress, not perfection.

It's time. Can we talk?

THE INTRODUCTION

There are not a lot of books that can speak with you, without assessment or conviction. Most speak to you. There are also not a lot of books that are intimate enough to resemble a face-to-face conversation that tap into some of your innermost thoughts, then sprinkle a bit of clarity, confidence, commitment, motivation and drive before gifting it back to you through a renewed and filtered lens.

THIS IS THE BOOK I WISH I HAD to help delve deeper into emotions I struggled to articulate and to help uncover a newfound confidence to stand up to limiting beliefs, when and where they formed.

It is our season to embrace, act, and thrive. It is our season to finally allow our courage to face our fears, then act in a meaningful and productive way. It is our season to marvel in creativity and leave footprints that guide others to find their "bolder" selves. We are standing on the foundation of a recharged energy - action.

Are you ready? I know I am.

I am Lolita E. Walker and I am four generations removed from slavery. Through a childhood story of my mom, her first cousin and my Grandma Bea, I am reminded that my great, great, grandparents and their ancestors have worked too hard, our families have sacrificed too much and countless others have endured too many ups and downs, to build the foundation upon which we each stand today.

NOW IS OUR TIME TO RISE.

It was the 1960's and the first year of integration at Forest Glen High School in Suffolk Virginia. She was only 1 of 10 African American students who were bussed in for an integrated education. Against, what she felt was her own desire and against everything she knew within her core, my mother, a frightened young girl, was reluctant to succumb to her mother's wishes. This, according to my grandmother, would be part of making history in these United States of America. Grandma Bea knew her daughter would be an element of something that never afforded her the same opportunity. With her daughter as one of the firsts within this inaugural class of integration, she would finally celebrate the wins of her parents, grandparents, and ancestors. She could walk into her own backyard of cotton fields to stand in the realization that this tiny break in history was finally here. Grandma Bea could feel the liberating power within it and marvel in its peace.

As she stood with her head lifted toward the sky, a smile wide upon her face and her eyes closed, she allowed the tears of joy, frustration, and fear to pour down her worn cheeks. The entrusted confessions, prayers, and future dreams. prompted her unapologetic release, as she stood in the arms of the field that she now owned. The thoughts of years she was made to pick cotton as a child, hands often pricked, prodded and numb reminded her of an education stopped short in the tenth grade. Her daughter was the piece of a puzzle who could and would complete the image of a little black girl amidst a sea of white children in her small town of Suffolk, Virginia?

To the contrary, my mother, Evelyn, pondered why God would allow this world to seemingly crash around her. One thing she did know for sure was that there was no second guessing her mother. Better said and plainly put, there was no talking back, going back, remembering back, or even attempting a flash back to restate her case AGAIN! This time tomorrow, Evelyn would be on a new bus, in a new school, with new people that did not look like her. They did not want her there.

She was TERRIFIED AT WHAT COULD BE!

What brought a small sense of relief was that she was joined by her cousin on her ride to school, which took two busses to reach their destination.

As the smell of homemade rolls filled the house on the morning of, Grandma Bea uttered a life-shifting delivery. "We were no less than anyone else. We were powerful. We were strong. We were phenomenal. We were worthy." She explained to my mother, in the calmest voice that she could muster, without crying, that you deserve everything that any of those children were born into. You deserve everything that God has destined for you. Grandma Bea made these professions and declarations, as she stared into her daughters' eyes, with an empathetic, yet steadfast look within her gaze.

Though being taught these lessons at home, my mother would board the bus with her cousin, with what felt like the world weighing upon her shoulders. Eyes gazed upon both of them, they walked into the school. My mom housed so many feelings. Anxiety, inferiority, panic, insecurity and fear, but according to Grandma Bea, she must always remember that her actions and her strengths are shaping a nation, whether it is felt now or in the future. She'd reminded my mom that some may call her angry, others may call her names. Some may throw obstacles her way, but Grandma Bea wanted her to know, little Black girl, you were made with love and strength. You are God's child and are a gift to this world.

At the end of this story, all I could think was, what if my mother, her mother, their mothers, and her cousin, could have read letters and poems that gifted them increased strength and confidence? What if this book was available to them? Would they walk, talk and behave differently? I'd love to say yes. Though I will never truly know, I have the powerful opportunity to shape a nation, with the gift of my words today.

May you enjoy the pieces within this book and may you leverage them, as needed, whenever needed, on your life's journey.

Can we talk?

This is to you, from me.
I love you,

Lolita

THE COMMITMENT

There will be times, while reading these letters and poems, you feel in an uncomfortable hot-seat. This is normal and you are not alone. Consider it a reflective moment, unlocking fragments of the innermost parts of you.

My Commitment to You

I, Lolita E. Walker, will journey with you and hold space for you.

Your Commitment to You

I _____, (insert your name) on the date of _____, am committed to giving myself space to read, reflect, and feel the power within my pause. I commit to allowing these words to penetrate areas that may not yet be unleashed within me. I commit to gifting myself all of me.

Signed: _____

Can We Talk?

Letters & Poems to Reclaim a Bolder You

DEAR
ADVERSITY

Dear Adversity,
Can we talk?

You dealt me some misfortune.
I instantly shut right down.
You thought I wouldn't see opportunity
to turn this here situation around.
Now, I must admit that I stayed for a while,
I was feeling so broken and so alone.

But,
It was then that I stood upon my foundation and
it was then that the sun finally shone
a light to my darkness,
where my internal chatter turned toward the left,
my affirmations curved right,
and my hardships -
they cascaded from the top layer that cornered me.
They cornered me like thieves,
searching for lost moments in the dark hallways of my mind.

Dear Adversity,
As I took a breath and counted from one to three,
my three turned to two and two turned to one,
as I won over the fact that you,
Dear Adversity, had none.
I remembered that I am me.
I remembered all that I am
and all that I bring to the table
because let's make no mistake -

I Am That Table.
I Built That Table.

Lolita E. Walker

They say that you, Dear Adversity,
are a 6-way tie that shatters spirits on the fly.

They say that you, Dear Adversity,
are the hardships that span the monotonies of life.
They say that you, Dear Adversity,
breaks down into:

physical, where unknown ailments dare to claim your space,
mental, which may hit you in the face
and limit the well-being that threatens your space.
Then there's emotional, that can dare to be freeing,
as I release control that I cannot control;
then social, because it's critical to the fabric of our human lives.
Then spiritual, where my faith gifts me an advantage over my life
and then there is financial, which can build a bridge
between where I am and where I want to be.

So, who the hell are "they,"
who want to house me in these six states of mind,
of being,
of seeing
all of me, Dear Adversity?

You came for me and as I face you,
I've taken stock of you,
overtaken you,
mistaken you,
so, I'm embracing you,
as an opportunity to do the right thing,
in this right now.

You've shined a light on the insights
that magnified the lessons
that you left on my table,
whether by accident
or you were voluntold.
The point is that I refuse to grab hold.

I acknowledge who and what you are
but I bid you and "they" a goodbye,
as I leap off to construct another table
that's big enough
to seat all of me.

Dear Adversity,
Can we talk?

This is to you, from me.
I love you,

Lolita

DEAR
ANCESTORS

Dear Ancestors,
Can we talk?

I want to thank you
for allowing me to tap into my ancestry.

I feel a supernatural connection with you.
I mirror a powerful reflection of you.
I hear a concrete direction from you.

I want to listen intently,
with my eyes,
feet planting into the earth,
I put in all of you.
Your voice dances in my thoughts.

You are my fore-fathers and my fore-mothers,
forced to disappear into hidden tunnels,
expected to funnel your voices
into the dark shadows,
to only become more invisible
under your master's watchful eye.

Your continued tries
to be treated equally,
in this one nation under God,
has notably leveled up my thinking -
my being.

I want to say thank you.

The eyes
that judged and misjudged you,
then raped your bodies and your minds.

Lolita E. Walker

The drums, can you hear them?
They are beating and beating.

The hearts
that had no beat of humanity,
yet pumped blood of hate and insanity.

The hands
that pounded into your skin
so that submission became the remission
of the teeny, tiny inklings of hope
that peeked from the sun.

There was a dare for you
to run to a freedom
that you were born to deserve.
Thank you, Dear Ancestors.

Our souls remain interlocked,
as your spirit raises from your grave,
with Golden Gospel Singers
who help you sing spirituals of
oh, freedom over me.
And before I'd be a slave,
I'd be buried in grave
and go home to my Lord
and be free.

Free.

Your tenacity

breathes life into my being.
Your strength
strings wisdom into my essence.
Your boldness,
it gifts clarity to my vision.

You, my Dear Ancestors,
have deposited grace into my emotional piggy bank
and have therefore
increased the value of my worth.
I want to say thank you.

I pray that I, and the generations yet to come,
will set and reset the pace of being limitless.
May we soar
beyond the heights of expectations,
hold on
to the traditions of family connection,
and bask
in the moments that become components
of a bigger we.

Oh, Dear Ancestors,
I see your tears.
I feel your pain.
I hear your drums.
They are beating and beating.
I see the markings on your skin
that permanently marked who was kin,
then shook the core of who you were
so deep within.

I want to say thank you.

Lolita E. Walker

And before I'd be a slave,
I will be buried in my grave
and then I'm gonna go home to my Lord and be free.
So, I want to say thank you for my freedom.

Dear Ancestors,
Can we talk?

This is to you, from me.
I love you,

Lolita

DEAR
ANGRY BLACK GIRL

Dear Angry Black Girl,
Can we talk?

Some misconstrue
how you show up.
This will never be me.
Your passion evokes a confidence
for what, where, and how
you deserve to be.

Stand boldly.

Break generational strongholds.
Dare to unleash the untold stories.
Re-write the typecast imagery.
Erase the culture that seeks
to victimize your super power.

You are worth more
than the categorization,
Dear Angry Black Girl.

Some will label you as "angry."
It will follow you wherever you go.
Some will treat you as an outcast.
Your greatness is beyond
what they have the capacity to
know
or experience.

Your fierceness supersedes the privilege
that you may or may not yet have.

Are you ready to grow?

Let's grow higher and higher
to a space we have yet to sow.
Let's plant seeds together.
Allow them to nourish,
as they flow like rivers,
as they narrow
to where assertiveness meets courage,
fierceness meets forgiveness,
and collaboration intersects with worth.

You
are a ball of insistence,
an intentional resistance,
a power woman who has created
an inward and outward fence.
You have already hurdled so many defeats.

You are standing right here.
These obstructions may leave a scar
and they are not for the weak.

Dear Angry Black Girl,
YOU are stronger than you even know.
The inequities and disparities
that you endure each day,
mounts with pressure and increased obstacles
that barricade your way.

They don't know
the emotion that spawns
from the passion that you feel.
They don't know
that this "angry black woman"
marches with confidence uphill.

What I want you to know,
as you read this,
in this moment,
right now,
right here,
is that you are a strong Black woman
who will no longer hide from fear.

Tell them to not assume who you are,
nor allow this stereotype to misguide their intent
Because you,
Dear Angry Black Girl,
are on a mission that is truly God-sent.

I want you to
walk with your head held high,
no matter the circumstances you are within.
Know who and whose you are
and from this,
you will not bend.

Then,
channel your "angry" to "action,
look them dead in their face.

Let them now
that at this pace,
this sassy black woman
that they don't even know,
will continue to shatter ceilings
and still help them to grow.
You will educate and empower,
still challenge the norm,

but to this label they want to attach,
nope,
you will never conform.
And you look forward
to taking this entire
world by storm.

Dear Angry Black Girl,
Can we talk?

This is to you, from me.
I Love You,

Lolita

DEAR
ANXIOUSNESS

Dear Anxiousness,
Can we talk?

Last night I couldn't sleep.
I tossed and I turned,
as my heart pounded,
like the drums of my ancestors.

My blood raced.
It filled my veins with the urgency
of now.
My mind fluttered.
I was fighting confusion
of what this war would and could be.

Would I build a legacy?

My lips curled,
as I asked God to lead me on a plight
to fight
for freedom.
My freedom.

Will my freedom ring from the mountain tops?
or fall in the rivers that flow from east to west?
I ask myself if I am doing my best,
Dear Lord.

As the light of the sun shone through my window,
I hear the chanting of my tribe.
I feel the intensity of now,
realizing that I am ready.

Can you smell the freedom?

Lolita E. Walker

On the other side of your mind
is a tribe that stands for you.

There is a war of words,
thoughts,
energies,
of my mind.
I am seeking to find
me.

With an army by my side,
my intention cannot hide,
my anxiety will subside
because my God is leading the way.

I check my intentions
And I smell victory.
The history of yesterdays
and the stench of ignorant ways.

My senses are on high.
I hear the birds sing with increasingly wild cries.
I feel the girth from the earth.
Can you feel it?
My birthright has begun to rise inside of me.

I see the fire across the land,
where we will celebrate the seven signs of completion.
I touch my neighbor
with the principle of Ephesians,
the unity of these bodies fighting as one.

I smell victory.
Close your eyes and breathe.

You are standing right here.

So, Dear Anxiousness,
Can we talk?

This is to you, from me.
I love you,

Lolita

DEAR
BLACK BOY

Dear Black Boy,
Can we talk?

I hear you
reminding the world
to say your name.
I hear the loneliness in your voice.
I see the fear in your eyes.
I imagine your mind spinning,
as you try to make sense of the lies
that are often misguided,
manipulated,
and falling short
of the whole truth
and nothing but the truth,
so, help you God.

I see you walking
with shackles of the world around your ankles,
as you try to ambulate boldly.

I see you standing
with an armor of strength and a badge of courage.
Yet there is a badge that has no courage,
following you as if you are inmate number 20032,
while walking in the freedom of this democracy.
What a mockery.

I sense the broken spirit,
hidden beneath the mask that you put on each day,
to navigate the haze of stereotype and judgement.
The haze.
The fog and the mist of darkness.
There is a renewed light.

Lolita E. Walker

Dear Black Boy,
I believe you when you tremble
from the whispers of fear
and the screams of doubt,
that threaten to cover you like a heavy cloak,
in the stillness of night.

I want you to know that
I love you.

Oh, Dear Black Boy,
I want you to know that,
it is during the times
when you pause and reflect,
that I am my most proud.

This is when I hear you lifting your voice to God.
And I sometimes see the water dripping from your eyes,
like the tip and tap of a faucet
that cannot be turned off.
In the darkness of your light,
I hear the silence;
the silence that overcrowds your space of discomfort.
Let me go.

I hear you.
I see you.
I see the presence
and strength of your ancestors,
who say your name,
with their arms extended
to lift you higher,
light you brighter, and

hold you even tighter.

Dear Black Boy,
one thing that I know for certain
is that
there will be times,
when deep down,
in the depths of your soul,
you will still hear the echo
and wonder
of a world that must change.
NOW.

I want you to know
that when I say your name,
I am always reminded of your
faith, strength, and love,
determination, pride, and sacrifice.

When I say your name,
I say it with purpose.
May you always do the same,
Dear Black Boy.

I hear you when you say that the world
doesn't show you that you are loved,
that you are worthy,
that you are deserving.
But Dear Black Boy,
God presented you
as a gift to this world.

May you remember
that you are greater than suffering in silence.

May you remember
that your voice is power
and there is power in your voice.

May you remember
that others do not define who you are.
Absolutely not.

You are the epitome of
greatness,
value,
worth,
and absoluteness.

You are bigger.
You are better.
You are bolder
than what any man or woman
can say
and will say about you.

Please look me in my eyes,
in this very moment,
to let me know that you hear me.
I see you.

Dear Black Boy,
please expect everyone to say your name.
Every morning when you wake,
I want you to say your name.
Remember the foundation on which you stand.
Rest atop of your values,
your strength,
your faith,

your uncertainty.
They will guide your steps.

Remember to surround yourself,
with those who can and will tell you the truth,
and lift you up when you are needed.

Oh, Dear Black Boy,
when fear threatens to overtake you,
please remember that fear is only an emotion,
that is powerful enough
to handcuff you,
your dreams,
and your expectations.

Fear is a powerful thing
that can be a sniper
and a bullet that aims to kill you.
Oh, but Dear Black Boy,
you must set and reset expectations
for everyone
to say your name.

And as you do,
You must remember the names of:
Eric Garner,
Michael Brown,
Ahmad Aubrey,
Tamir Rice,
Freddie Gray,
Trayvon Martin,
George Floyd,
Alton Sterling
and the many who go on and on.

They just remind me so much of you.
So, oh, Dear Black Boy.

When you say your name,
I want you to
say it with intention
and say it with purpose.
Say it with the authority
that you deserve.
The world will look at you with a different lens.

You will be hunted by words
and subliminal actions,
You will be profiled and targeted,
but Dear Black Boy,
remember that
you are made in God's image.
You must affirm your greatness.
Know it and believe it.

So, Dear Black Boy,
you may ask what I can do
to assist you on your journey.

Well, I -
I commit to hugging you
when love is what you crave.
I commit to gifting you help
and mentorship as you grow,
providing you a safe space to simply breathe.
Stand in your strength.
Say your name.

Dear Black Boy,
Can we talk?

This is to you, from me.
I love you,

Lolita

DEAR
BLACK GIRL

Dear Black Girl,
Can we talk?

You may have shown up today
with a heavy heart and a troubled disposition.
You may have doubt whispering in your ears
with a tone that seeks to instantly tear you down.

The fire that is inside of you
is yearning to be released.

Let

       it

              out.

You may have uncertainty
weighing upon your shoulders,
like a boulder,
simply too large for one person to move.

Oh, Dear Black Girl,
you may have anxiousness fluttering in your belly,
like a kaleidoscope of butterflies,
waiting to be unleashed.
Unleashed like a beautiful beast
who will soar higher,
and further and farther
than even you can imagine.

Close your eyes.
Allow the fluttering to take breath
within your beautiful mind
because you,
you look ahead
and only see obstacles of life
that have mounted before you,
before me.

Dear Black Girl,
This is before the world has yet to

see
      your
           greatness.

Oh, Dear Black Girl.

You may have felt fear tugging at your feet,
as you desperately try to forge forward,
in what feels like the thickness of mud
that is unyielding to your attempts.

You may have stood tall as you walked in the room,
then quickly bent back
to dodge the chatter, injustice,
unequal pay, hurt, and countless other daggers
that have been lodged your way.

But, oh Dear Black Girl,

      You
         Did
            Not
              Fall.

You may be tired,
as you hear another black and brown life taken,
taunted,
belittled,
or unrecognized,
in and around your space.

You gain strength from your faith.

Your ancestors will continue to lift you higher.

Oh, Dear Black Girl,
I've stopped by today to let you know
that you,
you are beautiful.
You are armored in God's grace
and you are infused
with the strength of generations before you.

Your chocolate skin emits a brilliant radiance
like no other.
Can you see it?

Oh, Dear Black Girl,
you are dazzling,
one of God's special gifts to this world.

May you always be reminded
that you,
yes you -
you shine brighter than any diamond,
even after it has been polished anew.

Be reminded that

You
       Are
              Worthy

of surrounding yourself with the support of a tribe,
who will quickly notice
when your cup is inching toward empty,
then rush to help you fill it up.

Oh, Dear Black Girl,
please understand that your community
acts as a defense
who recognizes, believes, and knows
that you are strength,
beyond what anyone can say
or what anyone has yet to see,
INCLUDING YOU.

Dear Black Girl,
I will help you carry your load.
You need only ask.

You are brilliant beyond where others
may try to set a boundary around you.
You are greatness,
beyond where even you can see.

Dream bigger in your betterment.
Walk taller in your boldness.

Oh, Dear Black Girl,
I want you to know that YOU,
You are the manifestation of greatness,
right where you stand
in this very moment.
The indescribable power that lay within you is
PURE MAGIC!

May you set your eyes beyond where they can see today.
May you know that there are endless possibilities within you,
simply waiting to be unleashed.

May you know that you are special.

You are enough.
You are light.

Keep shining for the world to see
and if for some reason, any reason at all,
you find yourself in doubt, uncertainty, and/or fear,
may you look in a mirror and say these words aloud.

There is power in my voice and my voice has power.
This time, please believe it, know it, trust it.

Oh, Dear Black Girl,
Can we talk?
You are me and I am you!
You are power, passion, and purpose.
May you always be free, live free, and love free.

May you
be you.
for you.
by you.

Oh, Dear Black Girl,
Can we talk?

This is to you from me.
I love you,

Lolita

DEAR
CHAMPION

Dear Champion,
Can we talk?

If I asked you to look into a mirror,
what would you see?
When I stare into your eyes,
are you committed to simple be
the greatness
that others have already told you that they see?

Was it received by you,
then cherished by only me?
Was it full of thoughts that limit your growth
and have you shackled
and surrounded by insecurity?

Do you see God's child staring back into your eyes?
Do you see the tears,
the hurt,
the pain,
the cries?
Dear Champion.

I am here today to let you know that
the beat is in.
The pressure is on.
Your time is now.
The champion in you has been reborn.

So, grab your win.

You've got this calling
to go all the way in.
Can you feel it, Dear Champion?

I see you putting in the overtime,
over time and time again.
I see you standing a bit taller,
raising your head a bit higher,
lifting your intentions
beyond where you stand today.
So, I want to play
in the greatness of your overlay
of motivation,
with a dash of inspiration,
infused with education,
which has become your core focus
that drives you
to the echelon of kings and queens.
It is obscene to think
that you would ever play small.

Dear Champion,
I stand here to remind you
that you are allergic to average.
It is time that we push even further and farther
than where you stand in this moment,
because time stops for no one.
It is time to rise,
victoriously.
You are standing in the winner's circle.
Can you see it?

I want you to dance
as if no one is watching.
Navigate the world
as if everyone will come knocking,
because they will.
Dominate your spaces

as if you said you couldn't.
Leap beyond boundaries,
as if commitment held your key.
Dear Champion,
it is time to rise,
victoriously.

This is your war cry.
Your heart's beating
and trying
to sit in the power of this pause.
Be energized.
The realness that is already within you,
it resides on the outskirts of your limits.

Who are you
to stand in the complacency of achievements
that you have picked up along the way?
Who are you
to lay down on others
who have not run their race
the way you say that they say?

Stay focused on you.
Don't be deterred by distractions,
that becomes petty infractions
of the whole you,
decimals that minimize the fact that
you are the numerator,
that sits atop the denominator.
You are worth more than the hashtags
that dare to define you,
and will raise
as an infinite measure of possibilities,

aligned with the presence
and essence of your survival,
in a world that is cruel
and tosses aside excuses,
as the tools of incompetence
that they are.
You are far more.
So, rise Dear Champion.

Imagine your inner beast being awaken.
Are you ready to grow?
The tables have arrived.
It is time to go boom and go bam.
Expectations, desire,
you were born for this race.
This space is the renewed place,
where you are building,
and growing,
and impacting.

So, Dear Champion,
we will rise together,
up like boulder, together,
and out like a phoenix, together.

Dear Champion,
Can we talk?

This is to you, from me.
I love you,

Lolita

DEAR CONTAGIOUS VULNERABILITY

Dear Contagious Vulnerability
Can we talk?

May the rising of these pages
spark the marathon in my pen,
that bends
and transcends
a multitude of notes
that float so effortlessly.
They yield uncertainty
in hopes of facing fear head on,
like my head is not straight on.

I
       must
           check.

The loneliness that flows
like water, with no destination in sight,
is the realization that

my
      plight
          is
               clear.
I pause
and I breath.

I breathe in the greatness of today,
I breathe out the negativity
that dares to come my way.

I scream NO.
You have no place in my line of sight.

Your intent may have gotten lost in the night,

but
        I
                stand
                        here.

I've cleared the fog
that wanted to stand right before me.
It wanted to crowd my space.
I stand facing fear,
head lifted to the sky,
heart beating and beating,
as fast as a NASCAR,
that attempts to bar me
from the endless possibilities
that are me.

Who is it that wants to claim this space?
My space.
Oh, but mi, fa, so, la, ti, do,
Ray sings back to me,
as I aim
to come face to face unconditionally,
then I dare you,
him, or she to stop my joy.
You are the essence and the depths of me,
the shadow that brings about the trees,
the stillness,
the beauty and what brings
about my most "be free."

So, I gift you my love, my want, my desire,
my touch, my loneliness,

my joy, my everything,
my, much needed contagious vulnerability me up
and drive me closer to that B side,
where the better part of me resides.

It's like you touch me and I catch you,
but this poetry palace has wings
to ignite this powerful thing
that throws me higher and higher
to an elevation
where my words are soliloquys.
They are poured out as batter,
then mixed, with no lumps,
sprinkled with a bit of power,
then infused with inspiration.

Add 1 cup of sugar-me-up
to the sweetness that I bring.
Add 2 teaspoons of bitters
because I have held on for so many years.
Add a dash of spark
and a dose to mark this place,
which we have allowed the sacred spaces
in, at this very moment.
And then stir well.

Let it marinate with courage
and bake on 350 degrees,
because well, my grand-momma said so.
And yes, we all know
that everything cooks just right
when you surround yourself with the right ones.
So, let's serve it up in a club with houses,
full of stages, that will

expose all of your Contagious Vulnerabilities.

God is moving in this place.

May my words have power
and may this power,
power my words
of vulnerability,
for being this courageous
and this contagious,
which has fueled the rising of these pages,
and have sparked the marathon of my pen.

Dear Contagious Vulnerability,
Can we talk?

This is to you from me.
I love you,

Lolita

DEAR COVID

Dear COVID,
Can we talk?

You are now part of history,
thus, you have spawned this in me.

I was once told
that a million seconds equate to 12 days
and a billion seconds sum 32 years.
So, add 44 years of my life
and see that I surmount all statistics.
Yet, I cannot fix this
infectious disease
that has infected me
and my 90 years young Grandma Bea.

You are the robber of humanity
that hooked my brother to his hospital bed
for five days,
in a misty haze
of tears,
as he struggled with oxygen levels
that had no gears
to level this playing field.
Yet, I still stand in gratitude.

I thank God
for the memories of those lives you've stolen
by your incurable, infectious disease,
that feeds our lungs with respiratory injections,
that reject the air that we were born to breathe.

A perceived mirror
reflects a treatment
that resembles a guessing game of "Guess Who,"
who desperately desires a cure

to help recreate our pure.

Help me help you.

Dear COVID,
there is nothing dear about you.

We've been molded to believe
that this momentary interruption
is created equally,
then distributed
and divvyed out one by one.
This side eye that you see from me
is for the blatant lie
you've spewed about this frightening beast.

We are predisposed to sugar and chronic disease.
We are cancer stricken and serious-illness restricted.
We must protect ourselves
and not move outside of ourselves,
for ourselves,
to gift ourselves the freedom of this thing called life.

Help me help you, Dear COVID.
You multiply through a discharge
that threatens to discharge the essence of humanity.
Where did you originate?
No, I mean really.
Where did you originate?

The origins of you are what I seek,
but why?
when the how
seems to level up and down like a sea saw,
that divides and conquers a mirage of flaws
within this pandemic space.

You've forced the creation of vaccines
that won't expunge the past or lessen the probability
that others will be engulfed by you,
but you jab and weave to infect me
with a portion of your potency.

It's the long haul of it all for me.

I was once told that a million seconds equate 12 days
and a billion seconds sum 32 years.
So, at 44 years of age, I surmount these statistics.
And yet, still I can't fix this.

I pray
to be vigilant in this.

Dear COVID,
Can we talk?

This is to you, from me.
I love you,

Lolita

DEAR DADDY

Dear Daddy,
Can we talk?

June 14, 2013.
It was the day my life shifted
for the better,
well, for the worst.
You taught me that God
won't grant us more than we can bear,
so, this curse,
I mean course,
that veered off track,
gave me a silent jolt
and then it forced me back
into myself.

I open my eyes differently.

I stood there
yearning to inhale
the many pieces of you,
the memories of you,
as I recalled all of the things
that I should have said to you
and wanted to say,
but somehow, they skipped me
in those last moments,
that I had with you.

I remember whispering in your ear
that everything would be ok.
I remember
confirming, then affirming
that when you were ready,
it was fine to let go
of this stay.

As a tear fell from one of your eyes,
I became aware
of the cries and tries
to be so strong.

They muffled
in the background of rooms,
filled with aromas of food
and fond memories of you.

But it was your smile,
Dear Daddy
that told the story.

I could feel the wisdom
of your 63 Jamaican years.
I could feel the irony
of my transposed 36
that lifted my tears.
In that moment,
I gathered my courage
and took flight
because God had flown you home,
Dear Daddy.

I felt the cues
of you infusing me
more and more
with the qualities of you.

There was the "he talks too much" gene
that allows me to talk to sold out crowds.
The "he writes too much" gene
that has me writing this to you
in my book number two.
"He listens to everyone's story,"

that has me hearing and pouring into others.
There was simply you, Dear Daddy.

There was the "we're going to Jamaica every other year,"
that gifts me appreciation for all that I have.
"You're going to college, but we have no money,"
that forced me to get off my ass.
"You've got more in you, my child,"
that elevated me to an MBA
with even higher goals on the way.
There was simply you, Dear Daddy.

There was the "we are allergic to average,"
that never allowed a "C" into our home.
The "no means no,"
that allows me to stand up in my greatest form.
There was simply you, Dear Daddy.

Your marriage lasted 38 years
and death did you part.
My marriage lasted only 15% of that.
Where were you then,
Dear Daddy?
We were unevenly yoked,
yet the yoke of me
was pulled out of me
and I needed you, Dear Daddy.

I've paved a new road
on my journey on this thing called life.

I am blessed to have had you
as God's child,
who was lent to me,
for only a limited, few miles,
in this lifetime.

I am grateful to have had you,
as one-half of the pair,
who has guiding me,
and molded me,
and shaped me,
what promises to be
a more expansive me.

I miss you, Dear Daddy.

I visit your grave and talk in the wind,
wanting and wishing you were there
beside of me.
The cancer that penetrated your body,
it permeated your cells,
and progressed to your bones.
It stood at attention
at stage 4, Dear Daddy.

Until I see you again,
I stand on this earth and I say,

Dear Daddy,
Can we talk?

This is to you, from me.
I love you,

Lolita

DEAR DIVORCE

Dear Divorce,
Can we talk?

I asked for you,
yet didn't fully assess,
confess, or regress
upon the ramifications of my ask.
Did you?

I expedited delivery.
A rush of emotions
questioned
whether you were hiding deep
already within the crevices of me,
of him, of we,
bubbling like a volcano ready to erupt.
There were the openings
that allowed pressures of circumstance
to pump through my veins and
the fracture,
the essence of who we were
together.

Did we slip through the cracks?

We were disconnected
from the links in the chain,
separated by the neurons in the brain,
and disassociated
by what was clearly unresolved pain.
Do you remember,
Dear Divorce?

Whether of a friend,

of a partner,
of someone we once knew,
you robbed me of the years
that I created so many memories.

When will I feel safe in this separation,
Dear Divorce?

We are here.
They are gone.
Friends, foes,
loved ones on the way.
That is ok.
I have opened up my doors.
I have let them off my train.
Now it is time for me to go
further and farther.
I am clearer.

The seats are opened up
and I am saying thank you,
Dear Divorce.
You gave me something
that I didn't know that I knew.
I didn't know that I needed.
I didn't know what would come true.

I am standing right here,
Dear Divorce.
And I say thank you.
God only gives us what we need at the time,
so, I thank you for rounding me out
time and time again.
I look back,

but then I am reminded
that you are standing right here.

So, once again, I say thank you,
Dear Divorce.
You separated me from
tears, and triumphs, and trials,
but put all together,
I know what I know
because I lean on
what will help me grow,
so Dear Divorce,
thank you for coming into my life
at the right time
and in the right place.

I am right here.

Dear Divorce,
Can we talk?

This is to you, from me.
I love you,

Lolita

DEAR EMOTIONAL MILESTONES

Dear Emotional Milestones,
Can we talk?

My emotions,
they tugged and they pulled
and sometimes they led me astray.
They held me and coddled me
when I needed it the most.
They found me to host
the shallowness of me,
the bright spots of me,
the endless possibilities
that I now see.
But, where was I?
I ask you,
my Dear Emotional Milestones.

I stepped onto the next milestone
and realized that they have loved me
when no one else was there.
They are me.
They've paved me,
as I experience all of my,
Dear Emotional Milestones.

I stepped onto the next milestone,
and the next milestone,
and realized that they, too, loved me
when no one else was there.
They are me.
They've paved me,
as I experienced all of you,
my emotional milestones.

You became stepping stones
that would lead to miles of open-air markets
within my mind,
within my soul,
within the tolls
of this thing called life.

These emotional milestones
would lead me to strength
and purpose,
to bloodshed and wars,
to sadness, to depression,
of lessons of tomorrow
and promises
of tomorrow's tomorrow.

Where was I,
when we kissed for the first time
and my tomorrows became today?
I tasted the curiosity that filled my mind
and helped me to make way.

I saw the blindness
that love had whisked away.
I, then felt my heart beating and breaking,
as the break of that taste
become bitter and less sweet.
You were gone and I sat in silence
for years.

My emotional milestones were here.
And I remember graduating from high school
and the pride that was in my daddy's eyes.
I remember the smile and expectations

that would force me to rise
higher into my mentality,
on what and who I could
become.

Then there was my first car,
first home,
first check that was bounced.
Were emotional roller coasters
going up and down and all around
my mind, my spirit, my soul?

There was the 1lb baby that was born
3 months before he was due.
There was my daddy,
who was stolen by cancer,
and I had no clue what to do.
But to move without grieving
was what came natural
for me.

There was the divorce,
that cracked the generations of marriage.
There was yet,
me.

There was the shame
and the forgiveness
that had yet to be won.
There was me
on an emotional milestone rollercoaster
that wasn't sent to me.
It was me.

Now my milestones mark my emotions.
My emotions fuel my pause.
My pause fuels the power that is me.

May my new milestones
leap me to my endless possibilities.
So, Dear Emotional Milestones,
I am ready for you.

Dear Emotional Milestones,
Can we talk?

This is to you, from me.
I love you,

Lolita

DEAR
FORGOTTEN ME

Dear Forgotten Me,
Can we talk?

Let's walk into this forest together.
I want to navigate differently.
I want to remember you.
I want to remember her, him, we, me.

Somehow,
I got lost in the domination of this forest,
but I still have yet to see the trees.
I want to remember you.
I want to remember emotion.

I want to feel your motions
and hear your sounds.
Those from the water
that tap,
and flow,
and glow,
in the wells that run so deep.
Those from nature
that whisk a cool breeze,
to freeze the moments,
that we spent together.
Those from me,
those from you.
Those that we weathered the storm
together through and through.

I want to hug the red wood
that is firmly planted into the earth.
So, let's unearth the essence of you.
Are you ready

to uncover
what you think has been forgotten?
You are not forgotten.
I see you.

I remember the drums,
as they beat
and as they picked up speed,
and slowed down,
with the resonance of your voice,
that hoists me higher and speaks so clearly,
and loudly,
without you saying even a word.

Dear Forgotten Me,
     let's
           move
               forward.

I see the colors of the leaves
that formed a seat
to catch me when I fall.
You did not fall
because I remember you.

I can't think backward
and won't dare to consider in reverse,
because, oh, Dear Forgotten Me,
you have threatened to erase my memories
that hang on the cliffs of fear and joy,
and happiness and pain,
and oh, Dear Forgotten Me,

What if the outpouring of you

were the emotions
that were pinned up inside of you,
simply waiting to let the sun shine through?

What if it were the right moment to unveil itself?
and then weave itself upon itself,
in the rails of expression,
by interlacing threads and strips and moments
upon itself?
Dear Forgotten Me.

The words of expression
want to touch you through a vibration
and it is so powerful.
Are you willing to receive?

Dear Forgotten Me,
Can you feel it?

You are invited to come with me,
explore with me,
transform with me,
as we run through the forest
and court this new free.
Let's finally grab that close up
with these trees.
Smile.

You are permitted to come closer
and follow the streams
that flow so amazingly
and weave into the veins,
the vessels of blood
that go into to my heart.

Close your eyes
and listen to these sounds.
Ding.
Ding.
Ding.
Ding goes the healing
and the sound of the bell
that rings so effortlessly.

To remember the lives that were taken,
mistaken,
now has me breaking my silence,
which has been covering me
for way too long.

I want to be surrounded by your release,
at the right time,
in the right moment,
in the melancholy of music,
that has hints and bursts of shimmering lights.
They are hints of purples and reds,
and blues and yellows.

Dear Forgotten Me,
Can you imagine it?

You held me like a mother holds a child
and all of me was cuddled
in a way that coddled me,
and opened me to feel all of me,
in the fullness
      that
            was

me.

I was and am
still buttoned up with softness
and zippered with vulnerabilities,
Dear Forgotten Me.

We are now able to shine through,
together.

I no longer feel forgotten.
I am not the blank pages in your book.
My pages are penned with honesty
and you are gaining the courage to flourish,
in a way that finally moves you to the front row,
my center stage.
Are you ready?
I think I see you.

What if you could make up the experiences
over time,
that held you back through intention,
and helped you let go of expectations?

Surrender,
Dear Forgotten Me.

The indigenous peoples in this land.
Your land.
My land.
My surrender.
Allow the spirit to move through you.
Through me,
all of me.

Dear Forgotten Me,
when all of our connections
have made room
for this royalty to show up,
even before your physical
blows up this room,
I want to thank you for holding my tears.

Let's walk into this forest together
I want to navigate differently.
I want to remember you
I do remember you.
Remember her, him, we, me.

Dear Forgotten Me,
Can we talk?

This is to you, from me.
I love you,

Lolita

DEAR
FUTURE LOVE

Dear Future Love,
Can we talk?

Do you dare
to hold me,
trust me,
extend through to my extremities?
Do you dare
to caress me,
lean into me,
become a one
with me?

Do you dare to become our "we?"

When we first met,
we showed up as two
with multiple do's and don'ts
and wills and wont's,
but
when we allowed ourselves to be free,
we made up the better me.
We've made this beautiful poetry
that bends,
and extends,
and transcends,
beyond the touch.
You've penetrated
my mind,
my thoughts,
my wants,
my limbs,
my whispers,
my me.

You helped me find me

and it feels so good.
We are intertwined
into a metaphysical space
that sets no pace.
We are here alone.
The world revolves around us,
but I am here with you,
and I love you.

From all of me,
from my soul
to the beating of my heart.
I love you.
I am you.

Be present
with the presence of us
and we,
and she,
and he,
and God
bless this union
that has engulfed us.
Allow us
to gift fruit to this world
that seats on the center of our bellies
and stays at the forefront of our touch.

I release me
into your hands
Penetrate me with your touch.
Listen to me beyond your ears.
See me,
minus the limits of your eyes.
Live through me

with a much-needed fill up
of what feels like the pure ecstasy
of my mind,
my body,
my soul,
my you.

The music we make together,
many may not understand
or dare to know,
but it is you and I
on the tippiest of toes,
sharing our woes,
and holding each other
in the process
of sea-sawing up and down
and down and up.
When you are down,
I'll hold you up,
when I am up,
you are invited to meet me there,
so, we hold each other down.

I love you.

Can you feel
this chemistry of trust
that is flowing in my veins,
extending through my organs?

You are me.
I am you.

I will not leave you.
You don't leave me,
because we are one.

Dear Future Love,
Can we talk?

This is to you, from me.
I love you.

Lolita

DEAR GOD

Dear God,
Can we talk?

I know
that you have made me
in the likeness of you,
but

      I

            am

                   struggling.

I am struggling to see greatness.
My greatness.

My circumstances
have created a home of isolation,
where the muddiness of this life
has threatened to slide me
deeper,
down a hole
and a hill of nothingness.

Dear God,
there is a group who look like chatter,
knocking at my window.
The world is peering in judgement
at my every move.
My soothing is now guarded
by large doors that are shut,
with no keys to unlock
the emptiness,
that resides within me.

I pray for peace, Dear God.

When I look into the mirror,

I see, what appears to be a blessing,
that is etched in the glass before me -
yet, remains foggy
from the steam
that fills me,
at every angry and frustrating moment.

Dear God,
as I look deeper,
I see a vessel
who is tired and worn down.
There are so many pieces of this broken child,
who adds makeup,
in hopes of masking the reflection.
My reflection.

Still, I stand feeling empty.
I pray for peace, Dear God.

I often feel betrayed,
irrelevant,
and passed over.
I stand,
knowing that there is more in me,
your broken child,
yet,
the energy to move
is simply too great for me to muster.

I fluster,
as I stand there knowing
and believing your word.
While I have seen so many small examples
of me in my greatness,
I feel so alone.

A lone ranger
with limited range to grow.
It feels so long ago
that I can remember
when things felt so amazing,
Dear God.

I keep asking myself why.

I trust and believe you
when you tell me
that I am filled
with the uniqueness like no other,
to love myself and my brother,
yet, there are times
when I forget
that there is a deep-rooted goodness
within the depths of my soul.

I am holding on to so much.
So, I pray for strength, Dear God.

I know
that you will not give me
more than I can carry,
but today, Dear God,
well today,
the load,
it seems heavier
than my shoulders can withstand.
I need you,
Oh, Dear God.

As I look at my reflection
and I pour more of myself into myself

and drizzle more of you
into me and my situation,
my lens becomes more focused
and I recognize that, wait...

I am
staring
at you.

I am a reflection of you,
Dear God.

I am reminded that my thoughts manifest into words.
My power has the words that are shaking over me.

My words have the power to leap into action.
My actions transfer into my spirit
And my spirit then fills the cup
of others.

Thank you, Dear God.

I am made in the image of you.
I pray for surrender, Dear God.

I am reminded
that I must hold my thoughts and my words sacred.
They have power to emit power.
They radiate with energy that blooms flowers
or cowers any man to their knees,
if we don't proceed
with caution.
And,
I know that this will not be the last time
that I feel this way,
but, Dear God,
here is what I commit to asking myself

when these thoughts threaten to overtake me.

If we were face to face,
would I profess limiting creeds
and negative thoughts directly to you?
Would I place the weight of my beliefs
and destructive words on your shoulders,
knowing how much you have already carried for me?

That cross, that weight.
Those words, those actions.
That unforgiveness,
that leads to forgiveness.
Oh, Dear God,
would I question if you were enough?
If you were worthy?
If you were in the right place at the right time?

Oh, this mind
that is constantly racing
and questioning
and forgetting
to trust you.
Dear God,
I surrender.

So Dear God,
I want to say thank you
for loving me just the way I am,
with my perfect imperfections,
within my reflections.

I mirror back the uniqueness of me.
I pray for surrender, Dear God.

Thank you for reminding me

that you have and always
will continue to hold me,
in the most threatening of times,
the most challenging of spaces,
even when the weight
seems too tough for me to bear.

I have come in contact with grace.
I feel your strength, Dear God.
Thank you for veiling
these blessings before my face.
I want to say thank you, Dear God.

Please help me to do the same.
You are me
and I am you!

Dear God,
Can we talk?

This is to you from me.
I love you,

Lolita

DEAR HEALING

Dear Healing,
Can we talk?

Sometimes I wonder if you are a person,
a place, or a thing.
I ponder if you are
this powerful notion,
that flows in the ocean,
like the waves
that offer potions
to remedy my soul,
my body,
and my mind.

Have I been blind to the sheer essence of you?
Dear Healing.

Are you a noun,
who met an adjective,
then romanced to birth a verb?
Are you a spirit,
who magically appears
when your name is being heard?
Please answer me, Dear Healing,
because I know that you're listening.

Can we walk down this path together?
break bread together?
move mountains forever?
Can we settle and nestle
under my favorite willow tree?
and allow our emotions to roam free,
as we dig
and explore the echoing,

yet fruitful depths of me, Dear Healing.

I have been longing
to embrace in this conversation for so long.

We now, finally have the opportunity
to sing this powerful song
of free-flowing dialogues
that excuse the monologues,
that minus the expectations,
sans the interruptions,
and are without the confrontations of life.

What if you could
restore my fond memories,
reconcile my brokenness,
and rectify my past?
What if this time,
I've finally found the remedy
that promises to last,
within you, Dear Healing?

What if you could be more
than this cartoon-covered band-aid,
that provides aid
to temporarily cover the extremities of my life,
that will completely strip me
of my inner strife?
What if you could act as the nurse,
who closely examines my wounds,
then pours peroxide
over my trauma-filled sores
to penetrate the cleanness
then you clean them deeply,

as you bubble from my inside out?

What if you
gently rubbed me with your ointment
and applied your special ingredients
to my soul?
You are welcomed to uphold
what God has created me to be.

My bout is not with you,
Dear Healing.

It is with the fear
on the path to get to you.
It is, in fact true,
that I must admit,
when I get out of my own way,
my path will be much clearer,
my vision will be much brighter,
and it will start
by inviting you into my world,
today.

Your therapy
acts as the masterpiece
that restores the plan
that you have already put inside of me?

Healing is an inside job
and I give you permission
to lead the mob
that shuts me down,
then bolts the door
and plays the episodes of my life

right before me.

May I stop looking outside
to smoke it,
to drink it,
to sex it,
and excuse it away?
For this play
is a new version of me,
that has been written
and directed
by you and I,
in this complicated duo of a ride.

Will you come uninvited
or shall I look for you in the mail?
Do you come down from heaven
or will you meet my horrific memories in hell?
Dear Healing.

Thank you for bringing this second chance
to regroup and balance
this soul-penetrating,
deep feeling
that keeps me kneeling,
hands folded under my chin,
looking to the sky
and praying to my God,
to help me grab the courage right before me,
because it's dangerous
to let your guard down.

But thanks to you, I am going all in.
Dear Healing,

I love you more than anything.
I suppose we all must heal

Dear Healing,
Can we talk?

This is to you from me.
I love you,

Lolita

DEAR
HEARTBREAK

Dear Heartbreak,
Can we talk?

When you grab hold of me,
you just simply don't let go.

Where do I start?

Is it the tears in my eyes
that surmise
the shattering of me,
in so many pieces
that have robbed me
of feeling the peace
that I need?

Is it the pierce that I feel
through this tussle
within this big muscle?
Is it that constant feeling
of a freefall in my belly?
Much like an elevator
that has been
cut from its cord.

The anxiousness
races from my toes,
to my mid,
to my heart,
to my head,
to the raptures
of you.

Breaking me open,

to ask whether my heart
can afford this breaking feeling
of betrayal,
forgiveness,
sadness,
and joy
that's wrapped all in one.

It was 10 years,
to barely 5,
then 1,
to none.

It was fun,
wrapped with sun,
in the sphere of its rising,
and setting,
and setting,
and rising.
The moon wraps its arms around us,
with a dim light that now watches
my light dim.

I paid the daily,
monthly,
and annual subscription
to you,
in full.

To your heart,
to its beat
of the same drum.

Can you hear it?

Can you feel it?

Boom.
        Boom.
                Boom.

But it shifted
to a different design.
Not the arrangement
of lines or shapes,
created from a pattern,
manifested from your heart,
but to the design of shared ego,
mixed communication
and pain.
The sharpness of its tip
is like a needle,
that simply refuses
to find its vein.

To darkness
and passing each other
in the hallways,
as if our hall
had a multitude of ways,
when we are
standing right here.

Can you see me?
Can I see you?

This closed-door feeling
is offering a strange,
yet cultivated escape,

through the hallways,
and backways,
and alley ways,
and mansions,
that we got lost in,
and the commotion and spaces,
with different lenses,
and the friends who weren't friends and the..

Hold up, wait a minute,
let me put some me up in it!

Let
      me
           talk
               me.
See,
forgiveness of you,
but really forgiveness of me,
because deep down,
I know that I have planted a new seed.

Dear Heartbreak,
I am grateful for you,
for all of you.

The ministry of my poetry,
this moment in me,
this flow that you see,
and hear,
and feel,
this is all of me.

This all of me

has a sista singing
and this sista is dancing
at the reality that here is now,
and now was then.

I am dancing,
and I am prancing
down the aisle,
as I stare at your son in his eyes,
as a tear runs,
and I race to catch it
before it hits the ground.
It wants to catch him.

In this moment,
I see all of his dreams
and those that's yet to come.
So, I weave in my imagination
and then
I tie a loose knot to hold him close.
I let him know
that he is more than a heartbreak.
He is the break
that is continuously set
and reset by my heart.

Oh, Dear Heartbreak,
you
      did
          not

 break

 me.

You offered me
a renewed me,
a better me,
a me that walks in to this different type of beat.
A single momma typa me,
a smooth co-parenting me.
A me that breathes deeply,
shares intently.

This me laughs contently
and is sitting in all of my agency.

Wait, I hear my doorbell ring.

Dear Heartbreak,
Can we talk?

This is to you, from me.
I love you,

Lolita

DEAR
LEGACY

Dear Legacy,
Can we talk?

I have two questions.
What do you want to be remembered for?
What will you be remembered for?

Now, before you answer,
please take pause.
Breathe with intent.
Allow with awareness
and proceed with fairness - to you.

The "what"
you will be remembered for
is a choice,
so, I offer you
the consideration
of the amplification
of your voice.

We know not the hour,
nor the day
that our physical presence
will leave this earth.
Unearthed
from the depths of this soul.
The roots
that dig deep in this lifetime.
I feel the root of your ancestors
nourishing this attachment
to this ground,
where these anchors,
and these fibers,
and these tentacles lay.

We know not the "how"

or the "where" our time will draw close.
It is on this day
that I want to hear you say,
that your innate gifts
are what make you, you.

Hold onto your faith, perseverance and values.
Stand upon your solid foundation.
Reflect upon the good
that I have done
and the footprints that I have left for you
in this sand.

Dear Legacy,
May you also remember the things I've done
that you dare not experience.
May you remember
that when you allow your natural
to become your supernatural,
that the world will feel the amazing
and unshakeable
boldness that electrifies
the pure power that is, you.

Dear Legacy,
you are mounted atop the fullness and strength
of your ancestor's shoulders.
May you remember
that they have faced their deepest
and darkest fears,
as they walked into battle
and peered upon the shadows
of their own deaths.

They toiled lands and withstood exploitation.
They pushed doubt and circumstance

to the sidelines,
that line the sides of actions and intention.
They drudged through trenches of hate
and injustice,
while holding their faith
in the palm of their hearts
and in their minds.

They nursed the scars,
as they mourned
those lost along the way.

Oh, Dear Legacy,
they, like you,
have conquered many enemies.
So, I want you to feel the power,
this power in your pause.
It is your pause.

May you continue to walk in your purpose.
Stand straight, shoulders back,
with commitment attached to your side
and confidence as your guide.

The world may not realize
your greatness right away.
Know that this is ok.
They will heed your words one day.

They may tell you
that you're not good enough
or try to use their words to ignite your fear.

So, Dear Legacy,
You are allergic to average.
We don't allow average to wreak havoc.

No.
Discouraged is a state of mind
that clouds the mind
to the greatness that it will find.
Keep maneuvering in your alignment
because straight is the path
that will avoid a wrath
and keep you seated in your foundation.

Dear Legacy,
may you know that tears
and heartbreak will come your way.
May you invite them to take a seat,
at the feet
of these moments.
Allow them to penetrate your depths.
When you have experienced them fully,
may you breathe deeply,
no less than three times,
then politely escort them from your space.

May you close the door,
as you hold on to the fond memories
and lessons therewithin.
Let go of the pain and hurt
so that when you fall,
and yes,
you will fall,
that you still win.

Why?
Because life is full of ups and down,
And twists and turns,
and scars and burns.
This will not be the first
and will absolutely not be the last.

But, oh, my Dear Legacy,
it is what you do that matters most.

So, I ask you right now,
What will you do?
How will you shift?

May you always remember,
that your words and your work
will leave imprints
wherever you show up.
Therefore, be intentional
on what you say,
how you say,
and the deliberateness
of when you say.

May it be on constant repeat,
that the fear
and mental instabilities of others
do not define you.
Instead, may you use them to
fuel you.
Allow them to walk with you
on this rocky path called life.
You were born from generations of strength.

So, Lord,
please bless my legacy
and power the centermost point of his life -
this life.
Forever grant a trinity of bold blackness,
unapologetic power,
and a spirit that serves you,
Dear God.

May my legacy not be misunderstood,
and broken by a system,
who won't hold him tight,
yet threatens to lock him up,
on this very night.

To my legacy,
you are beautiful.
You are strength.
You are love.
You are heard,
seen,
and
recognized.

Dear Legacy,
Can we talk?

This is to you from me.
I love you,

Lolita

DEAR
LIMITING BELIEFS

Dear Limiting Beliefs,
Can we talk?

Do you believe in miracles?
This is an invitation to close your eyes.
Imagine the birds,
that fly across the skies
of endless possibilities.
Imagine the ocean
and its motions
that float
and flow so effortlessly.

Can you see it?

That miracle of blues and greens
that roll so limitlessly,
with no end in sight.

Can you feel it?

That miracle of this life.
That burning in this moment.
That passion in this time.

Can you imagine it?
Can you now imagine you?
I mean, I do.

I see you moving,
and flowing,
and glowing,
and wait,
it's not all rosy and bright.

There will be rough highs,
and low, low tides,
There will be ins and outs on your journey,
when the world feels
that there is no one around,
when you feel lost,
and there is no sound,
of inspiration or motivation.

It's in those moments
when the showers of adversity pours,
the thunder of depression roars,
the way forward is not clear anymore.

Do you remember that?
I do.

I also remember that
God is in this place,
manufacturing our renewed space
for healing.

You are a miracle in motion.
Are you ready to receive?

That extraordinary manifestation of breaths,
that breathed a thousand times,
with confidence as your guide.
Your mentality has the power
to crack the tragedies
that so often cloud your mind.

It is your turn to touch the sky.

You are a miracle in motion.
Your proper preparation
has prevented your poor performance,
so, you stay prepared
to reframe your perspective
of the mundane,
turn it into magic,
and pull
your future rabbit out of your hat.

Take inventory.
You are the narrator of this here story.
You must shake the comfortable
to get uncomfortable,
to become a new typa comfortable
and then let folks go
who you are not there for,
and who are not there for you.

Let them go.
They are not on your miracle
and spiritual highway.

Can you feel the miracle inside of you?
Because it is you.
Doubt and fear, you no longer live here.
When you gift yourself permission
for your natural
to become your supernatural,
you begin to level up
in the most intentional of ways,
to meet those history makers,
those status quo breakers,

and take-charge kinda takers,
that lead this one nation under God.

Be that motion in the ocean
that floats and flows so effortlessly,
with that miracle mentality
of showing all the way up,
because when you know what you know,
then you trust where God says go,
you believe in what you've sowed.

You are absolutely ready to receive.
You are a miracle in motion.

Dear Limiting Beliefs,
Can we talk?

This is to you, from me.
I love you,

Lolita

DEAR
LOST FRIEND
(PART I)

Dear Lost Friend,
Can we talk?

It was last summer
that was our last summer,
together.

Hot days and mysterious way.
Tiny talks
that branched into longer walks.
Fireside chats that burned all night.
And secrets that we vowed to hold tight.

We were supposed to be together,
forever.

Had I known
it would be our last summer together,
I would have fallen into the spring
and frozen the winter cold.
I would have hugged you a bit tighter
and not taken for granted
that we'd grow old,
together.

It was the last summer
that was our last summer.

I long for the day I see you again.
Until then,
I have thoughts of the summer
that didn't get away.
You will always give way
to the best of me.

I remember you
because you were here
for our last summer.

Dear Lost Friend,
Can we talk?

This is to you, from me.
I love you,

Lolita

DEAR
LOST FRIEND
(PART II)

Dear Lost Friend,
Can we talk?

I never wanted a war.
I never asked for a war.
A war between you and me,
a war between the efficacies
of our minds,
and what we wanted and deserved,
and poured out and poured in,
and then,
the real kicker was when,
you allowed us to be pulled apart by them.
How could you?

They stood at attention
with guns of hate blazing,
and jealous-filled bullets,
grazing the sides of my soul -
the beating of my heart.
They forged forward,
with anticipation of winning
in their bones
and a false portrayal of safety
in their homes,
and felt like thorns in the back of me -
in the union of we.

The tones from their tongues
were waving the "let's get it in" flag,
because they thought
that I had no one to come in for the save.

They were wrong.

You thought wrong.

Their intentions,
covered you like a helmet,
influenced you like a virus,
and put the crush on us like a plague.

Dear Lost Friend,
I never wanted a war.

You thought I would clamor
into a cave of depression,
with a regression,
that would take me back
into the place,
where you thought I needed you
more than I needed me.

You came ready for me
when I had forgotten about the real me,
so I couldn't
necessarily see
what was happening right before my eyes.
I blame me.

I never wanted a war.

But now the conflict that I see
is that we are on two different pages,
on two different stages,
and now I done gone back
to that single stage of me,
that is backed with the arsenal that I need
to succeed in this here war.

I never wanted a war,
but you came ready for me.
Your militia came ready for me.
I never wanted a war.
But we are here.
So, let's go to war.

I've not yet called in my calvary
because they'd be here momentarily,
but I stand planted in the earth right here,
looking into your eyes
and wondering why I didn't
see the disguise of who you truly were,
who you truly are.

I've packed my war bag
and read the *warning, warning*
you've got only a moment
before I grab my knife
to cut you with these words
that are wrapped-up
with hidden swords,
'cuz you came for me.

Lunches in the city
with so-called friends,
late nights on the phone
with your so- called man's and 'dem.
Yes, I asked for you to go.

It's only a moment
before I pull the pin from this grenade
and throw it back into the fields of shade

that you gave me
so, you walked right past me.
Where was the real me?

It's only a moment,
before I wrap you in this baggage,
of your yesteryears,
and your non-committal ways,
and non-confrontational ways,
to meet me up here,
where your greatness never soared,
where your potential never roared,
where you having my back was a thought,
that obviously was swept up,
with the scraps on the floor.

But then I woke up,
'cuz it was all a dream.
I am a bigger and a better me.
I am a forgiving,
yet not forgotten me,
and living in the fact
that
you'll never have another one of me.

I never wanted a war.
You will always be at war,
because
you can't stand up for the soldiers
that have your back inside of this war.

So Dear Lost Friend,
I am here.
You are there.

Dear Lost Friend,
Can we talk?

This is to you from me.
I love you,

Lolita

DEAR
LOVE

Dear Love,
Can we talk?

I'm struggling
with what you really look like to me.
I've recently come to see
that you are a complex recipe
of do's and don't,
of shoulds and woulds.

You are an encompassing spirit
that fills my spirit.
I love you,
Dear Love.

I walked into a room
and saw you standing near the door.
It was open,
yet closed off to the world.

It was closed off to me
because I'd yet to fully see
you.

I swear I heard you say
that you simply wanted more
from me,
from the depths of within me.
I couldn't fathom that this was true,
Could this really be?

You looked me in my eyes
and then realized,
that I'd poured out
all of my emotions,
as you stood there

and pulled at its strings.
You stuck a dagger in my heart
and acted as if we were just a fling,
then you recoiled
and sent me right back.

You watched me fall apart.
In those moments,
you seemed not to care,
but on a dare,
you called me when those
moments were over,
and under and over,
and side to side,
Oh, Dear Love.

I want your help in redefining
and recommitting to what
and who you are.
I want to feel you
and hear you.
I want to taste your sweetness
from near and far.

I want to overdose on the freedom
that drips from my tears.
I want you to caress my body.
I want you to tap into my fears.

When I imagine love,
I imagine you.
When I imagine you,
I imagine me.

Dear Love,
What if?

What if you are chaos and amazement?
What if you are big and gentle and warm?
What if you are open?
and gasping for air and transparency,
and yet you still felt like home?

What if it had no order and no plan,
yet still hugged me like a perfect tee?
What if,
Dear Love,

Do you really want to be here for me?

What if you were protection
that pushed us outside of our zones?
What if you were the sun on my skin
that was longing to not be alone?

What if love were you,
Dear Love?

What if you were patient?
What if you were kind?
What if it took the opportunity
to finally fill my mind?
I feel you.
I felt you
throughout my entire body.
What if it took you over
and simply penetrated my soul?

What if love had no barriers, no egos, no friends.
What if you had no family crowding your space?
What if you were able to look me dead in my face?

Lolita E. Walker

Would you?

Dear Love, do you feel my love?
Have I overstayed this visit
that is here with you today?

What if love was laced with fear?
Would you turn back
or would stay planted here with tears?
Would you drink from your own well?

Love is just plain hard.
Well, not true
if you pull the "be all in" card
and do it naturally.
When you allow trust
and invite yourself
to love unconditionally.

This is hard.
It hurts so beautifully.

I have figured out the key!
It is loving all of me!

It is leaping with risk
of where I don't need to pretend.
I am gifting all of me.
I am blessing you with me,
Dear Love.

Thank you for your twists
and your turns.

I am coming for you.
God is love
and I am made in His image,
so, I am love

Dear Love,
Can we talk?

This is to you from me.
I love you,

Lolita

DEAR
MEGHAN

Dear Meghan,
Can we talk?

Are you silent?
or are you being silenced?

That was the question
that Oprah asked you so eloquently,
as you sat poised so intentionally,
with your confidence
dripping like pearls,
as they adorned your black dress
and white embroidery.

I remember
that you were backdropped,
with a landscape
that escaped your former land,
then you invited us aboard your journey,
with honesty and authenticity
as your game plan.
Then you navigated us
along each path,
every step of the way.

You were on cruise control
that was only powered,
with the permission to simply say
exactly what and who you are.

Thank you, Dear Meghan.

For it was in those moments
that I imagine she could hear
and see the pain throughout your story,
that was selfishly for me

and selflessly for every other being,
who was eager to see
you uncover your eyes
and gingerly unfold
the permission to yourself,
for yourself,
by yourself.

It was as if you were
unwrapping and unrolling
years of multiple trolls
to finally gift yourself your story
that had yet to be told.

It was
your own narrative
that was imperative
for the world to hear
in your eyes,
in your words,
in your time.

Once a feeling of unprotection,
turned gratification,
that transformed
to your protection
of freedom,
with pro-voice and pro-leveling up
in the most American way.

Thank you, Dear Meghan.

Are you silent?
or being silenced?
That was the question
that Oprah asked you so eloquently,

as you sat poised so intentionally,
with your confidence
dripping like pearls,
as they adorned your black dress
and white embroidery.

I,
like many other women,
have sat in the darkness,
where there seemed to be no light.
I,
like many other women,
have felt unprotected,
and have experienced fright.
I,
like many other women,
have felt trapped
by some sense of the word,
whether mentally,
spiritually,
physically,
emotionally
or any other -ly that one can imagine
or fathom
or bring enough havoc to or through.

See, I,
like many other women,
were seeking to shine a light
on the old version of me
but hadn't been successful at seeing me.

Where was I?
Where did you find you, Dear Meghan?

You were chased with thoughts of suicide
that would not subside on their own.
When you asked for help,
everyone turned their backs,
as if no one was home.
You had more questions than answers
and this was more like a cancer,
that fought like hell to shut you down.

But not you, Dear Meghan.

It was when I looked at you
that I saw the hurt that was in your eyes.
It was when I felt you
that I felt the isolation
that was squeezing you on all sides.
It was when I heard you
that I heard the strength
that was within your voice.
It was when I reached to hold you
that I was cradled
with what I recognized was your choice
to show up in all of you.

Shattering the status quo,
with your husband by your side,
your hands interlocked,
and head lifted toward the sky.
You looked at each other,
then you gazed at each of us in our eyes,
to once again,
give voice
and narrate the edits to the pages
of your book.

You erased the words
that others deliberately wrote
with systematic hate.
You backspaced over the letters
that offered no context from the gate.
You added spaces
that deserved your pause.
You bookmarked images
that elevated your cause.
You found and rewrote you,
Dear Meghan.

Have I said thank you, Dear Meghan,
for showing up in all of you?
Have I said thank you, Dear Meghan,
for owning your truth?

See,
there were so many nuggets
and lessons and gems
that were dropped, but today, Dear Meghan,
you represented the headlines and bylines
for all of the powerful women
who have ever entered my space
and they dared to share their stories.

It was the, *"I didn't know what I didn't know,"*
that first drew me in.
It was the, *"yes, I am a Black woman,"*
that gave our culture it's next win.
It was the, *"speaking with intention and with grace,"*
that pulled me right along.
It was the, *"vulnerability of it all,"*

that prevented any perceived risk of a downfall.

It was the, *"I've got my husband by my side,"*
that punched them dead in their eyes.
It was the, *"we built this thing together,"*
that proved that your love would last forever.
It was the, *"how dark will your baby be?"*
that dug deep for me.

And through it all, Dear Meghan,
you stood in all of your excellence.

What truly did it for me was the,
"my mental health is worth more than any institution."

That right there.

It created a powerful new fusion
that, if I were to have a crystal ball
that granted me only one wish,
I'd see King Harry and Queen Meghan
upon the throne,
correcting parts of history
that were worth being overthrown.

It was a free masterclass for me
that was evident in its entirety.
When a man loves a woman,
when a woman loves her mate,
there is something rare that occurs,
no man shall ever penetrate.

Dear Meghan,

Can we talk?

This is to you, from me.
I love you,

Lolita

DEAR
OPPRESSOR

Dear Oppressor,
Can we talk?

I woke up with a heavy heart,
knowing that
you were coming
for me.
You were coming for me
and my people too.

I look at you
and I stare at the hate
that you see in me.
I can feel it.
Both literally and physically,
you are
stabbing that dagger into my heart.
I kept my composure,
my head is lifted,
hands by my side,
my fists are tightly balled,
yet steady.

I am ready for you.

I will rise.
I am made
to surprise the expectations
that have been placed upon me,
by this world.
I am the world.
You have been warned.

I close my eyes
to find the love
that must be within you.

Lolita E. Walker

I search myself
for the forgiveness
that must exist
for me to move on
for me to forgive you.
to forgive me,
to forgive we.

My brows are arched,
with inches of skepticism
that haunt my mind.
They push me to grind
harder.
deeper.
reflectively.

I am ready for you.

I will rise.
I've built the chains
that dare to frame my neck
and my movements.

You have been warned.

I am here,
Dear Oppressor.
You have found
the empty crevices of me,
that you
and your hate
have yet to penetrate.

I will not let go.

My access is sacred.
My prayers have strength.

I will not let go.

My eyes are opened wide,
yet they remain unphased.
My nose is slender in stature
and wide in sniffing the BS
that blows a whiff my way.
My neck is slender
and poised upward,
knowing that I will
see you coming here.

I am ready for you.

The bondage that you hold me
is deafening.
It is threatening.
As I look beyond you
to the struggle and strife
that is bigger than me.

It is my people
who remain unfree?
How can this be
the reality of today
and the promises of tomorrow.
I choose to look beyond
and rely on the greater me,
the intentional me,
the God set in me.

The newspapers
that color me with headlines,
they curve at my bosom

and fit me like glue.
They attach themselves to me,
as though they are the color of my skin,
the essence of my kin,
the loveliness of the shades that are me.
I am shouting
how I have been forced
to comply to the rules
and I am challenging
the way I come to the table.
Because I have built this table.

The red, the white and the blue
that covers my dopeness,
that brings my freedom,
can you hear it ring?
They dare to shackle me
from creativity.

I am ready for you,
Dear Oppressor.

I will pause.
I will feel my own power.
I am love.
I am leaning into you.
I am leaning on you.
I will survive you.
I have survived you.

What do you have for me today,
Dear Oppressor?

I do flips in the city
that is now broken up

by your craziness.

But, Dear Oppressor,
I am here.
I will not move.

Dear Oppressor,
Can we talk?

This is to you, from me.
I love you,

Lolita

DEAR PEACE

Dear Peace,
Can we talk?

Hate
surrounds us like a cloud of haze,
and humanity has become unfazed
at senseless murder,
which has taken up space and time
of our thoughts
and our hearts.

My mind spins,
as I see black and brown lives taken
and taunted.
My heart bleeds.

Is there room for you, Dear Peace?
Is there space to reach
a higher plateau,
while we are here on this earth?

I am tapping,
and beating,
and listening,
for a cadence of harmony,
in the midst of a world
full of chaos & greed.

Grab my hand.

Move with me,
then pause with me.
There is a stillness
that brings a collectiveness

to penetrate our souls.

I can feel it.

A boldness of energy
fuels my most be free
and allows the world to see,
differently.

I dance as if no one is watching,
feet grounded,
eyes closed
and moving to a beat
that is my own.

Can you see it?

What if we could grow our Dear Peace?
Attach it to the earth
as a planted seed.
Allow its roots to grow
as a collective of wonder.
Water it with tears of yesterday.
Feed it with sunshine of tomorrow,
then watch it blossom
into a collectiveness of
inner & outer peace.

I want you to
flow with me,
with us,
with we.

Dear Peace,

Can we talk?

This is from you, to me.
I love you,

Lolita

DEAR PERFECTION

Dear Perfection,
Can we talk?

Are you wound
in a ball of expectations,
that are laced with
what she said,
and he said,
and you said?

Are you a square
of imperfection and rejection,
of what you rinsed and washed
and then fed to my brain?

Are you masked as a triangle,
with an oddity
that grants serenity,
so that I may think
from whence you have come?

I am you, Dear Perfection.

I remember
my daddy
telling me
that I was allergic to average,
and moving forward
was the only path to my play.
I remember
the look
of pride and achievement
and the affirming words
that he would say.

I remember

my mother,
beaming bright at my accomplishments
and pushing me harder
if I didn't get it right.
I remember
the love being poured
when she saw me give my best fight
for knowing that I had truly done my best.

See, the rest,
is the pressure
that I put on to myself,
for myself,
by myself,
because the movement of progress,
for me, will never be put on a shelf.

I am you, Dear Perfection.

Our relationship
is one of being free
because I deserve all of me.
I shook off the shame
that I once held on to
for being your friend in the open
for everyone to see.

I apologize for pushing you to the side
and speaking ill toward your name.
I am you,
because I am made
in the likeness of you,
Dear Perfection.
I claim you
because you created me,

and I created you,
and I want the world to see
and experience the depths -
all of it -
that you curated me to be.

Now, oftentimes I fall short,
but
what I do know
is that I am worthy
of unleashing the potential
that is buried deep
within the soil of my soul.
What I do know
is that I will continuously grow
more toward your light,
so, Dear Perfection,
please grant me the wisdom that I will need
to help guide me
to be more free
and increase my humility,
as I express my fragility
and release my vulnerability.

I aim for you.
I claim to you that I am you,
Dear Perfection.

Painted as a perfectly imperfect vessel,
as I navigate this thing called life
through and through.
I've found the person
that I was intended to become,
destined to gift from you.
My passion has met my purpose

and then has collectively
and abundantly
ignited my power to be.

On those days
when I don't feel like you,
Dear Perfection,
may I just remember
that love starts with self
above anything else.
The journey is to perfection.
It is that perfection and polishing yourself anew.

Dear Perfection,
Can we talk?

This is to you, from me.
I love you,

Lolita

DEAR
PURPOSE

Dear Purpose,
Can we talk?

Sometimes,
I feel as though you hide in plain sight,
yet,
I can't feel from your eyes,
this form of a light,
to shine on the fullness of me,
visually.

Sometimes,
I see you shining so brightly in others,
yet,
I can't see the flicker
that ignites a flame,
to exclaim the nuances
that proclaim my worthiness.

Sometimes,
I hear you dangle bits and hints
of what you are and I wonder
if the rings and chimes of your essence
are the presents that sing promises
of sweet nothings in the night,
unleashing what you have hidden
within me, Dear Purpose.

What if
you were the narrative
that told the story
of how I could pour into others
the way that others have poured into me?

What if
you could grab a peek
into this ritualistic bookmark
that marks the pages of the unwritten books,
that I've yet to retrieve
from my mind?

What if
you were the alignment
that drew the lines that, one day,
merged at an intersection on the verge of
serendipity spaces and surrendering places?

What if you were already within me,
Dear Purpose?

You know,
that butterfly that flutters in the pit of my soul,
You know,
that friend who unfolds, then folds, then refolds,
the innate gifts
that get displayed
and then told
so evidently,
so effortlessly.

You know,
that thing that is undoubtably God-given
and dares to be driven
deeper and deeper
and further and faster by me,
for me.

Dear Purpose,

here's what I've come to the realization of
and have been flooded with full recognition of -
you have absolutely shown up in me.

You are that captured fish, who,
when released, swims so certainly and so freely.
You are that creativity that emits the light,
that when I hit the switch to engage you,
you engage differently.

You are that destiny
that I am living in right now,
the timing that is divinely being found,
the living that pushes me to the corner,
then affirms that accountability is your middle name,
with ownership as the frame,
who positions me
to travel and journey about your
Purposeful Pathway.

So, Dear Purpose,
I am here for all of you.
I now submit to fit into free-flowing spaces
that erased expectations from others
and quite frankly from me.

It's not a question of why I hadn't found you,
but more so, how I inadvertently stumbled
upon my greatness that was always right here
to bear witness to me leaping over the fear
of finding you.

I've now grabbed you by your horns
to hone in and hold on,

to uncover the plate that has fed me with success,
has clothed me with choice,
and hugged me with ambition and conviction,
then peppered me with dedication and aspiration.

I want to say thank you
for dosing me with your rhyme and your reason,
because now you have helped me to find my season
that encompasses and explains my why.

I am selfless when I am walking beside of you.
But it is because of you, *honey,*
that I am that shimmer and that shine, *honey*
that passion and that grind, *honey,*
that hope
that will find,
those who are ready and willing to receive all of me
and my purpose-filled passionate specificity.

So, Dear Purpose,
Can we talk?

This is to you, from me.
I love you,

Lolita

DEAR
REFLECTION

Dear Reflection,
Can we talk?

It is Sunday.
The standard day
to pour all of my sins away.
I pray
and ask God
if today will be the day
that
everyone sees the real pieces of me.

The sun shone on the chapel steps,
as I see the women
parade into the churches
in their extravagant hats.
I walk in.

From the pews,
I look ahead
and finally make room
to close my eyes.
I'm struck
in my soul
by the souls and their voices,
which pour into my heart.

The popsicles of life,
in all of their colors
and shapes and flavors
they are so rich,
as they drip down into my spirit
and cover me
like the stickiness

of trials and tribulations.

The bitterness fuses with the sweetness,
then lines my lips with a hallelujah
for me being on this earth yet another day.

Dear Reflection,
I am here.
I see you.

Dear Reflection,
Can we talk?

This is to you, from me.
I love you.

Lolita

DEAR SADNESS

Dear Sadness,
Can we talk?

Sometimes, you cover me like a blanket
and smother me so I can't breathe.
Sometimes, you threaten to pull all of my joy
and the greatness
that is already within me,
from places that I dare not visit on my own.

You clutter my mind
with words that add no value,
but instead,
they sink me
into this space
that is not worthy of my time,
my energy,
my space.

Dear Sadness,
you are simply not worthy of me.
Sometimes you push me into a valley,
where the water flows
out of my eyes like the river.

Today is the day that I overtake you
with a life raft of joy and calm.
Today is the day that I look inward
to use your power to dry up my tears,
that threatened me,
as I cower in fear.

Yes.

Today is the day that I

wipe
away
you.

Dear Sadness,
I am surviving you.

Sometimes, you push me into a cave,
where the water flows through the cracks of its foundation.
Sometimes, you push me into a valley,
where the stream flows from my eyes,
like the ice flows from the glaciers.
But in this sadness where I sit,
I want you to know
that I've learned so much about me.

My tears of sadness
have now manifested
into tears of gratefulness
and for that,
I can now see the light.

I am grateful
for where I stand in this sadness,
for being here and saying this aloud,
for what I do have
and what I don't have,
for this space I find myself today
in this ray of sunshine
from where I am speaking
to me,
from me,
in all of me,
Oh, Dear Sadness.

My tears have now become keys

to unlock the darkness,
behind the door
that was this loch ness monster for so long.
They unlocked the door
that was adjacent
to the cave that you tried to stick me in,
Dear Sadness.

You live and you love to find me everywhere.
But watch me turn my frown into a smile
and this smile into the life and strength of you.
You just wait,
Dear Sadness.

You are not all together bad.
You are so much more than a fad,
as you come and go
and disrupt the flow of this thing called life
my life, my life, my life, my life,
I am looking for sunshine.

When I am sitting,
and staring,
and glaring,
and conversing with you face to face,
so many who love me
want to quickly usher me from your space.
But why?
I am love.
I am unbothered.
I am your survivor.

I am sitting in all of you,
which allows me to sit in all of me,
so why not just allow me to simply be,

Lolita E. Walker

Dear Sadness?

You see, this emotion
sometimes feels like an ocean
of fear and anxiety,
and excitement and joy,
at the same time -
at least for a while.
So, when I'm ready,
I'll grab my smile
and let go of you.
Until then,
I am sitting in this pause to say,

Dear Sadness,
Can we talk?

This is to you, from me.
I love you,

Lolita

DEAR SILENCE

Dear Silence,
Can we talk?

I hear you
so loudly in my head,
expressing
what I am unwilling to speak aloud.

This cloud of consciousness
is deafening,
as it hums
a flatline,
in line with my thoughts
and my actions.
They are holding me captive.

Please free me, Dear Silence.

I stand on this stage
speechless for an audience
of many
that may carry burdens
for some
and a blanket of innocence
for more than just one.

In the still of the night,
my eyes are open
but I hear nothing,
I see nothing
in this darkness
that fills the night,
that blinds my sight,
that offers me this pause.

May I close my eyes
and feel the power
that is in this pause
that you have offered me.

Thank you, Dear Silence.

You've offered me a stillness
that I have been so afraid to take on,
I will trust you.

I will grab your hand
and walk beside of you,
as I leap, Dear Silence.

Please be unapologetic in your approach.
I appreciate all of you.

Dear Silence,
Can we talk?

This is to you, from me.
I love you,

Lolita

DEAR
SINGLE MOMMY

Dear Single Mommy,
Can we talk?

Let's be clear.
You've fought through
an enormous amount of fear
to be standing right here,
today.

You held up the earth
with a different typa strength.
You muscle through mud
that we didn't even know existed.

You hold the universe
of the world on your shoulders.
Thank you, Dear Single Mommy.

You carry the wants of your children,
the expectations of your work,
the demands of yourself,
and still,
you stand strong.

You weigh the words
said and unsaid by others,
as you move throughout this world
and also resolve
that there is a fault
in something that you have said
or you have done.

No, Dear Single Mommy.

My Single Mommy,
Your eyes can cut a room
with one stare.
I want you to know
that you
are one of the strongest humans
that I know.
I listen to you cry some nights
when you think that I am dead asleep.

I see you
sorting through bills
and wondering if everything will be ok.
I see you
hanging in food pantry lines
telling me
that you picked up groceries
on your way home.
It is ok, Dear Single Mommy.

You are more than enough.

You have kept a roof over all of those heads
no matter what you were doing
or where you were going.
You kept food in their mouths
and clothes on their body.
Now they are older
and they recognize that, wow,
this was not an easy task.

You even challenged me
when I wasn't feeling at my best
and didn't hesitate

to talk to teachers
or parents
and move mountains
whenever -
whenever I needed.

Oh, but Dear Single Mommy,
the sacrifice of it all
is that
you are standing right here
with a smile on your face.

It is time to rest, Dear Single Mommy.
You do not have to bear this alone.
Look around.

It's the conversations that matter most.
It's the things we want to say and we simply don't.
It's the release of you to the release of me.
It's your words,
your emotions,
and you filter all of me.

Are you finding you, Dear Single Mommy?
I love you.

Despite all my broken parts,
you believe in me, so I believe in you.
You trust in me, so I trust in you.
You are loving me, so I love you
Here is a hug from me, to you.

Dear Single Mommy,

Can we talk?

This is to you, from me.
I love you,

Lolita

DEAR SISTER

Dear Sister,
Can we talk?

It was months ago
when I closed my eyes.
I imagined you reaching down for me,
lifting me up from the ashes
that I often find myself buried within.

I feel you,
tugging at my hopes and my dreams,
as you dared to mirror them
right back to me.
I saw you,
as you carefully prepared to glue
the broken pieces of my yesterday
and erase the cloudy glimpses
of my tomorrow,
Oh, Dear Sister.

I want to say thank you.

It was weeks ago,
that I reached back up to you,
yet,
the distance between our touch,
it resembled decades and centuries
reclaimed and reclaimed,
as they penetrated the innermost parts of me.
Where were you, my Dear Sister?
I needed you.

I want to say thank you, Dear Sister.

It was days ago
that God sat me still
so that I may finally feel
the whirlwinds
that I was the mastermind of constructing,
the tornados
of chaos
that I had a voice in agitating,
the pot
that I stirred
and quickly moved to the setting of high.
It instantly became this boil that bubbled over.
My top had fallen off.

The steam from my attitude
fogged the gratitude
that was right before my eyes.
It replayed the blessings
that it had already poured all over my life,
then it retouched the blemishes
that marked the child
that I once was.
It became the doctor,
who prescribed the remedies to my soul
and then grabbed hold
of the essence and presence of His Glory.

It made me
realize that
I needed healing, Dear Sister,
yet,
I projected all of me onto you
and you became my issue #242
but,

where was I, Dear Sister?
I had lost myself within myself
and needed to jolt up
and step out of myself.

I wanted to say thank you, Dear Sister.

It was because of your whispers in the night
to others about me
that didn't become
more and more,
that have shifted me
into the best of me.
It was the renewed me,
who can now reach back
to see
that you are
my Dear Sister.
And for that,
I want to say thank you.

I forgive you, Dear Sister.

Because of my God,
I have moved beyond my ego.
I have pushed that to the side.
My tone has been atoned
and I've given birth to the newness
that was waiting
to be unleashed within me.
It is today
that I am calling on you, my Dear Sister.

Will you lend me your hand, once again?

Will you lift me higher?
Will you walk with me
down this clarity cul-de-sac,
as we repair
what we have said and unsaid,
what has been cast as an outcast?

In James 4:11, we are told, Dear Sister,
not to slander one another
or speak ill of one another
because in doing so,
we stand in judgement of God's law,
so may we release our flaws
and become the sisters
that God has intended us to be.

If not by blood, then by might.
If not by might, then by sight,
and His word.
Can we agree, Dear Sister,
that as I clasp my hands together,
it is for you to lean in
and lean on.

It is for you, Dear Sister,

It is for you to lift you higher and higher,
and further and farther.
So, I vow to collaborate, not compete.
I vow to remember
that two are better than one
and a collective is better than some,
so, let's march together forever
and be the children

that God has always intended for us to be.

Dear Sister,
Can we talk?

This is to you, from me.
I love you,

Lolita

DEAR
SUCCESS

Dear Success,
Can we talk?

It was a memory of the yesterdays
that had me lay in the abyss of you.
It was the promise of the tomorrows
that had me re-imagining that
this could really be true.
It was the hues and the rues of your taste
that prompted me to close my eyes
and suckle on the sweetness of you.

You are success.

You frighten me.
You heighten me,
You sometimes threaten me.

You are so bitter
and so pleasurable
at the same time.
You are grapes of the finest wine,
but somehow got lost in time
of others' expectations and realizations.
I've gotten stuck on the vine
and my palette is somehow intertwined in chaos.

Please open your mouth
to grant me
my all-access pass to you.
Don't chew me up
and spit me out, Dear Success.

Instead,

allow me to explore
the innermost parts of you.
Your cheeks emote honey
from the comb of progress,
and create
the imperfectly crafted wavering of choice.

The gaps in your teeth,
they grant permission
to weave through the strength,
to bite off more than I imagine
that I can even chew.
I want to taste more slices of this life,
of your life,
Dear Success.

Please help me stick to the roof of your mouth,
so that you cover me with my values
and umbrella me
with the after taste of wins,
that I've claimed along the way.

You are success.

You breed remnants of taste
that I invite to stay.
You coat my belly,
where the butterflies reside,
where the fear is set there to leap.

My goals are molten in gold
and if poured over me,
would run through
the crannies of my soul.

You are welcomed to stay here, Dear Success.

I am blessed and highly flavored.
Can you taste me?
'Cuz I can taste all of you.

You are success.
You are my success.
I am radically persistent.
I am tasting all of you.

So, Dear Success,
Can we talk?

This is to you from me.
I love you,

Lolita

DEAR
TAKING A STAND

Dear Taking a Stand,
Can we talk?

We are standing
in a pit of mud,
that sinks
lower and deeper
into an abyss of hate,
that is chained
by loops of bias,
and anchored
by steel and doubt.

We are standing,
to combat the injustice
from the system of justice,
that weighs on our necks
and our backs,
and took the life
that was already so exhausting
so, Stand Up.

What if
I was standing?
but
standing could cost me my livelihood,
that seats on the foundation
that holds our families afloat.

We,
have eyes in the back of our heads
for fear of not knowing
or seeing what is before us,
around us,

beneath us.

We,
have additional arms to grab hold
of the privilege
that others use to push with disgust,
and mistrust
for what is assumed
that we are bringing to the table.

We,
carry the weight of the world,
the freight of our nation,
the uptake of our people.

Steeping unearthed coffee
that came from the earth,
that paints cocoa to cover my skin,
my melanin.

What if we choose to take the mask off
and stand up?
Take my people with me,
together we will thrive
and not jive and shuck
for a dream
seen through a microscope.

Offend the stereotypes
and Stand Up,
because we will disappear
into an abyss of absence,
covered by the showers of bullets,
the stench of hate,

doormats of swastikas,
that strangle us with sheets and whips.

Can you feel my pen?
It is running away,
as Harriet helps me to
stand up?

Stand up.

I feel it in my bones,
my veins,
my miles
that I have travelled
on the backs
of those that toiled this land,
with the bitter,
yet distant sands.

I want to hear the drums
beating to a distant beat,
I want to see the markings
on their skin,
screaming who was their kin.

I want to embrace the strength
of knowing
that we were born from generations
of kingdoms,
full of kings and queens
who walk this earth.

Submission.

Stand up and take me with you,
my head is bloody
but it is unbowed,
with a gun of courage at my side.

Unloose the shackles
because it's time to
Stand Up.

Run.
Don't walk to the nearest opportunity.
Leap over struggle.
Marinate in triumph
and then grab the victories.
Beat down any obstacles.
Shatter ceilings.

Look at yourself in the mirror
and see me,
see us,
see we.

STAND UP.

Dear Taking a Stand,
Can we talk?

This is to you, from me.
I love you,

Lolita

DEAR
TODAY

Dear Today,
Can we talk?

I am in desperate need
of pouring out what I feel
in this moment.

I am tired.

Yet,
I continue to show up
with a face of strength each day.
Can you see me?

I am speaking,
yet others choose to hear only silence.
Can you hear me?

I march to a beat that is my own,
yet,
I find myself trying to keep the beat of others.
Can you feel me?

Dear Today,
when I dig deep
and pull the honesty from my belly,
I must admit that,

I

      am

            ready.

And because it is only you and I in this space,
I am owning my truth.

I am speaking it aloud.

I have come to the realization,
that I have secretly
been comparing myself to others.
Have you been there?

I have been taking stock of their wins,
while diminishing my own.
I have seen little reward and recognition
for my ongoing contribution.
I now realize
that comparison is the thief of my joy,
Dear Today.

As I reflect in this very moment,
I want you to know that
I see you.
I hear you.
I appreciate you.

Dear Today,
May I ask you to let go of yesterday?

This could be the yesterday
that was my today minus one
or this could be
a mirage of yesterdays ago.

May I ask you to remember,
that despite your struggle
and your situation,
that taking time to reinvest in you
is a much needed AND deserved place to be?

May you erase the guilt, fear, and doubt
that is banging at your front door?
May you sit in this pause
until you are able to shift
to the best version of yourself?

Dear Today,
May you remain present
and sit within your presence?

Why?
Because you are enough.
You are worthy.
You have earned a place at this table,
my table,
your table.

Dear Today,
I am loving all of your newfound glory.
I am loving the flurry of greatness,
that whirls like snowflakes in December.
I see you
with your arms stretched so wide.

You are twirling around,
head lifted to the sky,
as the snowflakes hit your tongue.

I see your inner child
being released and finding new moments to smile.

Dear Today,
I will no longer borrow from tomorrow

to feed my today.
What if you, Dear Today,
were my last today?

May you always remember
that you have the option
to press the restart button.

Begin this day
renewed.

Dear Today,
Can we talk?

This is to you, from me.
I love you,

Lolita

DEAR
TOMORROW

Dear Tomorrow,
Can we talk?

I don't know what you will bring
or what you have in store.
I've closed my eyes to leap farther,
to become your something more.

I see myself.

My future self
is staring into the distances
of bolder dreams yet realized.
The unfamiliar and not yet understood.
The shoulds and coulds that await you
to dream beyond today.

I'm hoping you'll bring a change of pace.
To help me asses the race
of comparison
to yesterday and today.

I pray we quickly meet face to face.

Dear Tomorrow,
May your light shine brightly
to illuminate my way.
May your path offer curves
that gift choices beyond today.

Dear Tomorrow,
I know that you're not promised.
I vow to live every day like it's my last.
But what if I vow to push my limits,

To leap beyond my past?

What if,
I vow to not chastise,
those who did me wrong,
day in and day out?
What if,
I vow to be my most authentic self,
and not get lost in fame or clout?

Would you then promise to bring me more tomorrows?
What if I were you and you were me?
Where would we be?

Dear Tomorrow,
Thank you for being the light
that illuminates the path before me each day.

Verbs are the actions
that merge our yesterday and today.
And, Dear Tomorrow,
I've left footprints along our way.

Thanks for helping me vision the opportunities
of living my highest and most intentional self,
as I future cast myself
to shift into my whole self.

I pray that
I continue to see
my hopes and dreams realized.
I am moving closer toward you.

Close your eyes.

I am standing right here.

Dear Tomorrow,
Can we talk?

This is to you, from me.

I love you,
Lolita

DEAR
TRIALS &
TRIBULATIONS

Dear Trials and Tribulations,
Can we talk?

The trial began.
The gavel hit.
The eyes peering on my soul
and reaching beneath
and beyond
me.

Do you swear to tell the truth?
The whole truth
and nothing but the truth,
so help you God?

Who was this woman
putting on this façade
of strength
through her trials
and tribulations?

It is judgement day.
I breathe in.

With the judge and jury
looking to judge with fury,
with the prosecution showing up
more than my defense,
can I build a fence around my tribulations,
so that I may breathe
and nourish my soul?

My adversity.

I was dealt misfortune,
yet,
opportunity still stood right up ahead.
When I was feeling broken and alone,
who was there to lift my head?

These trials.
These tribulations.
These rejections that slap me as I sleep.

Turn off the chatter button.
Clear your head of the noise,
that wants to crack the whip of limiting beliefs,
that has cornered you on this witness stand.

Wake up.

You are standing right here
in this right now.

May the hallways of your mind
flip the trial on its head,
tell the tribulation
that enough has been said,
and grab back the voice
that God has given to you.

You are made in His image.
So, may you stand on the foundation
that grabbed the breadcrumbs of misfortune,
the bag of trials and tribulations,
the tote of adversity,
and knock it on its head.

May this momentary interruption
bring the best of you,
to the rest of you,
because adversity becomes a distraction
when the world awaits you on this day.

Dear Trials & Tribulations,
Can we talk?

This is to you, from me.
I love you,

Lolita

DEAR
UNLEASHED POTENTIAL

Dear Unleashed Potential,
Can we talk?

Hey there.
I didn't realize that you were right there
beside of me,
inside of me,
and let's be honest,
I didn't realize that you were handcuffing me
at the same time.

Hey there.
I'd love to invite you to spot
the intensity of my unleashed potential.
Today, I unlock the imaginary shackles to my mental,
as I stencil these words directly to you.

The pins and bolts
that are holding me,
are now bolting me,
to unearth my inner unleashed potential.

Hey there.
How did I walk past you
and not see you standing right there?
Blame it on my mind and not on my heart,
that is beating
in anticipation of you,
Dear Unleashed Potential.

It was as if you were
hidden in those back rooms
that gave room to nooks and crannies.

You know,
that room where everyone knows,
but dares not to go.

You know,
that room that is hidden in plain sight.
You know,
that room where the lingering souls
paint up and down the walls,
as they lay a canvas
to portrait me, as I feed you,
unleash you
and wipe the cobwebs
from your brow.

I thank you for being so patient,
Dear Unleashed Potential.

This morning,
as I look at the foliage on the trees,
they sit in their stillness,
so restlessly.
And I choose me.

With courage by my side,
I see my Dear Unleashed Potential.

The oranges and browns
gift cedar to crowns,
that fuse reds and purples
to help me see my Dear Unleashed Potential.

The shades of burnt orange
and sun-kissed colors drew me in,
as the sun kissed a permission slip
for me to simply pause.

I hear the loud banging of thoughts in my mind.
They threaten to overpower me with complacency.
I feel the relaxing of my head, as it lay back.
I harness the energy within me,

wanting to release me,
unconditionally.

This potential is about to break me wide open.
Are you ready to witness then experience the explosive me?
3, 2, 1 – I go BOOM.

I concentrate on the wiggle of my toes to free up my woes.
They have been your sidekick for way too long.
This kick in my belly is demanding so much attention.
Can you feel it?

Hey there.
As I swallow my energy
to travel back up to the dome of me,
I faintly see the cage
that I put around my being.
I am seeing that my energy was caged,
literally.

Are you my Dear Unleashed Potential?

What if I unlocked the door?
It turns out I have always had the key.

So, hey there.
I didn't realize that you were right there
beside of me,
inside of me,
and let's be honest,
I didn't realize that you were handcuffing me
at the same time.

Dear Unleashed Potential,
We could have died together,
but after today, we are riding together,

in the sunny of yesterdays,
today and tomorrow.

You still shine brightly,
yet,
this time,
you are in my rear view.

I address you accordingly,
from the driver's seat.

Dear Unleashed Potential,
Can we talk?

This is to you from me.
I love you,

Lolita

DEAR
WARRIOR QUEEN

Dear Warrior Queen,
Can we talk?

At the end of your daily battle,
I see you sitting atop of your throne,
where the sun has shone
for years,
and decades,
and centuries.

Your smile,
sometimes finds you alone
in what
can feel like the wilderness of
atonement,
for your millions of yes's
and your handful of no's.

Your woes,
have created holes
of inconsistency
and complacency,
Dear Warrior Queen.

I see you.
I am you.

I hear you when you say that
the world's pressures are squeezing you,
the distractions are mounting you,
the stillness
and the cold,
they take hold of your dreams,
as they cut,
like falling glaciers into the earth.

Will you catch them?

I hear you when you say
that you've been trudging,
and grinding,
and finding yourself
at the same merry go round and round again,
Dear Warrior Queen.

I want you to breathe
and walk into your dreams.
Breathe in the greatness of today
and the opportunities
that are right here in your way.
Do you see them?

Unpack your bags,
Grab your courage,
Pick opportunities up
and move them along.
They are waiting to be found.

Because you will heal a nation.
You have healed a nation.
Stand up.
You are Warrior Queen.

I hear you.
I see you.
I feel you,
Dear Warrior Queen.

I have heard your battle cries.
I have, too, experienced the tries,
as you've rised so abundantly.

Fix your crown.
then grab hers off of the ground.
We walk this thing called life together.
We lock arms forever, so that
when your sister is down,
you pull her up
and when she is up,
you fill her cup.

Remember that you are at the forefront,
facing front,
with scars on your back
and visions out past tomorrow,
so, Dear Warrior Queen,

Knock out the bears
and the lions
that dare to crowd your space.
Scream with the loudest boom
that goes bam.

I feel your heart beating,
and racing, and pacing, for spacing,
and places that pace you back and forth,
with the worry and doubt.

I feel a supernatural connection with you.
I mirror a powerful reflection of you.
I hear a concrete direction from you.

So, who are we
to not shout
from the mountaintops

that you are a Queen?
We are Queens.

Please allow me to help fix your crown,
Dear Queen.

You are being seen today.
You are being felt in this space.
You are being held.

So, Dear Warrior Queen,
Can we talk?

This is to you, from me.
I love you,

Lolita

DEAR
WISDOM

Dear Wisdom,
Can we talk?

I look beyond the trees
to dream bigger,
to vision more boldly.

I close my eyes
and allow nature to grab hold,
shaking the torments of yesterday
and creating space
for the promises of tomorrow.

I
listen
intently.

Dear Wisdom,
I long to hear the melody within your voice,
as you whisper in the wind,
chime in the distance,
and extend your knowledge to me,
for me.

Thank you, Dear Wisdom.

The spirit of my ancestors surrounds me.
They cover me
with the blessings of yesteryears,
of years of trials and tribulations,
hurts and tears,
of wavering strength,
of conquering fears.

You will stand,
says Dear Wisdom.

May you help me stand in the presence of now,
get lost in the experiences
that I allow,
in
my
space.

May you be the calm
that politely plows
distractions from my way.

Thank you in advance, Dear Wisdom.

I plant my feet deeper into the earth,
and become present to the moment,
in all of my intentionality.

The weight of the world
is slowly lifting from my shoulders.
My burdens are like boulders,
pressing into the extremities of me.

Dear Wisdom,
Will you pour into me?

The height of the redwood trees
are reminders that
I am stronger than I know,
with massive potential,
ready to steadily grow,
Dear Wisdom.

But what if I showed up in all of me,
Dear Wisdom?

Would my roots intertwine
to form a community of strength?
Would they stretch wide,
go deep,
and lift us
the length of perpetuity?

Dear Wisdom,
Why didn't you tell me
that there was
this indescribable power
within my soul?
The type that gets released
when I choose
to simply
pause?

My superpower
emits the pure magic
of all who I am
and all of who I will become.

Far beyond where my eyes can see,
Where my mind can imagine,
where my thoughts can fathom,
Dear Wisdom, why didn't you tell me
that we're each here for a unique cause?

A mission and a divine purpose
that birthed us.

Lolita E. Walker

We are beings
that live free and limitlessly,
Dear Wisdom.

I look beyond the trees
to dream bigger,
to vision more boldly.

I close my eyes
and allow nature to finally grab hold,
shaking the torments of yesterday,
and creating space
for the promises of tomorrow.

I
will
listen
intently,
forever.

Dear Wisdom,
Can we talk?

This is to you, from me.
I love you,

Lolita

DEAR
WRITERS BLOCK

Dear Writers Block,
Can we talk?

I seem to have a bad case of you,
Dear Writers Block.

Somehow there's a piece of my brain
that simply won't unlock,
the words and the images
that I know you put on hold,
the creativity and imagination
that are still waiting to unfold.

There are letters that make up words in my head,
that jumble at the thought of being read
in public spaces,
with places that judge
and become the judge
of my dear vulnerabilities.

As they dance,
I lose the focus of perspective,
and see images of a collective
of nothingness.
My objective is lost
in these blurred letters
that aim to complete the sentences
that are you.

They are blurred letters and poems,
written as a child.
They are forgotten talent that was lost,
and I now long to find
the melodies that are unsigned.

The rawness of talent sits within me,
yet, Dear Writers Block,
you have yet to unleash
my creativity.

Oh, Dear Writer's Block,
how dare you show up right here and right now.
There's so much I want to say
but somehow,
I just don't know how.
You have grabbed me so tightly.
I almost want to scream.
It's as if I am stuck in a dream.
Dear Writers Block.
Well, I'll take a nap,
then walk the block once or twice.
Please throw me a life line.
Anything will suffice.

Maybe a word, a thought, an image, or a vibe.
Maybe a note from a bird,
a magician in the sky,
or a dance from a tribe.

Oh, Dear Writer's Block,
you've got me this time.
I'll give you that small win,
but may I please ask that you
release my brain
so that I may begin.

Dear Writers Block,
Can we talk?

This is to you from me.
I love you,

Lolita

DEAR
YESTERDAY

Dear Yesterday,
Can we talk?

I've made a hard decision,
to let you know,
that after
what seems like forever ago,
I have decided to let you go.

My emotions took the form of a shadow,
that lurked in the creases of my mind,
my body,
my soul,
my you.

You hid in plain sight,
like a blanket,
covering me from head to toe.
I've decided
that it is time for me to go.
I've mustered up the courage
to free myself.

Let's take this trip down memory lane,
switching over the broken yellow lines,
with signals that threaten to cloud my mind.
Oh, Dear Yesterday,

Do you remember
how you jolted me aboard a roller coaster ride?
Elevating me to a massive high
and filling me with love and laughs?
Do you remember
that when I finally reached that pinnacle,

you held me there?

Then you dropped me
to the lowest of valleys
that housed sadness and tribulation.
That vibration that jolted the essence of me,
the fullness of she,
the fullness of we.

You will not hold me,
Dear Yesterday.

I hadn't quite realized how attached I was to you.
It was astonishing
just how many memories
flowed to my mind,
through my mind,
above and beneath my mind
and ultimately left me blind
to what was right before my eyes.

I immediately began to clear the cobwebs
in a fit of overwhelm, but
the over is whelming me
deeper and deeper into your space.

Dear Yesterday,
I found hidden spaces
filled with tears and circumstance.
Others were refuge for joy and celebration.
I now see the light.

I now know that this nation awaits my voice.

Dear Yesterday,
you do not have permission

to hold me in this moment.
It flows free of torment.
I want you to know
that in every corner,
I grabbed a memory.
I hugged myself with wins,
clothed myself with faith,
and looked in the mirror
and I saw all of me.

My gratitude has fueled my attitude.
You've given me the fortitude I need to push on.
So, today I simply say Thank you, Dear Yesterday.

I found that I was living in the shadow
of what was and what could be.
I was holding on to the "potential of."
I grabbed hold
of what I thought you could and would be.

You are not invited to see my today.

I'm no longer available
to join you on that same roller coaster ride
time and time again.
I listen to the doubt and fear
that you cast my way.
Dear Yesterday.
After thinking long and hard,
I've decided to let you go.
I am shaking the cobwebs,
I am closing the door
and looking forward to tomorrow.

I'll grab the good that you've offered

and most of all, Dear Yesterday,
I forgive myself.
I forgive myself
for the struggles and hardship that I created.

Dear Yesterday,
I forgive myself
for not accomplishing
every single thing I possibly could.
I forgive myself
for holding on to you
for so long.

It's been a long journey
but we are parting ways today.

I
am
reclaiming
me
and
I am looking forward to tomorrow.

Dear Yesterday,
Can we talk?

This is to you from me.

I love you,
Lolita

DEAR
YOUNGER ME
(PART I)

Dear Younger Me,
Can we talk?

I remember you.
Do you remember me?

Do you remember the days
when we had no cares in the world?
Do you remember the street lights
illuminating reminders
of five minutes to make it home?
Do you remember the ice cream truck
playing a familiar song
that alerted everyone
that the time was now?

I remember the
wow of your first kiss,
and the bliss of magic
in that very moment.

I remember the torment and the cries
when friends and relationships waved good-bye.
The heartbreak
and closed doors
that would unlock the deadbolts
to author new poems.

I remember your anger and frustration
resulting from your parents' strict ways,
which became fundamental gateways
to navigate the maze
of pushing through
to discover the bolder, you.

.

Your newfound cheerleaders
led the cheers of leader ships
that you would later sail across the oceans,
of space,
of time,
of triumph,
of shine.

Dear Younger Me,
I remember the sacrifices you made,
as you inched more seasoned in your age.
There were follows for follows,
as you followed everyone else's lead,
yet,
struggled to find and follow the seeds
that had already been planted just for you.

I remember your first raise
and how quickly things changed
in your mind and in your spirit.
You were gifted
a renewed perspective
on life.

You realized
that you'd been raised
by parents,
who raised you higher
and wider
than this whole world
could and would ever do.

There was the first stamp in your passport

and your travel overseas, alone.
There was the internal phone
that you called as an SOS
when you were stressed.

There was the ability to pay
your parents' way,
without debt overshadowing their stay.
I remember the pride in their eyes
and the words that you would say,

Oh, dear child,
You will shake a nation.
You have shaken a nation.
That's what they said, so
Dear Younger Me,
I remember the memories of it all.
Your coping, then moping
with your first reality of death.
The emotions penetrated the depths of you.

Dear Younger Me,
Do you remember questioning
your value,
your worth,
your impact?

Well, I am standing right here.

Please always remember
that I see you.
I feel you.
I am you.
I thank you.

I thank you for challenging all of my triumphs.
I thank you for the mistakes and the failures,
the laughs and the smiles.

I thank you
for listening, then doing,
for being, then loving,
for simply being - you.

For without you,
I would not be the amazing person
that I am.
For without you,
I would not be the amazing person
that
is
you.

Dear Younger Me,
Please help me to remember all of those moments,
the good and the bad,
the happy and the sad.
The memories that grant these soliloquies
are holding me to a more esteemed me,
so, I say thank you, Dear Younger Me.

Please help me to stand upon my greatness
and make the future-me proud.
Please help me to speak my stories aloud,
so that I may help others stand out from the crowd,
because they have not yet experienced your wow.

I am me because of you.

Do you remember?

Dear Younger Me,
Can we talk?

This is to you, from me.
I Love You,

Lolita

DEAR YOUNGER ME
(PART II)

Dear Younger Me,
Can we talk?

I've dropped by today to let you know that
your evolution will be televised,
broadcast for the world to see
on screens that grow with inches and
dare to expand through yards of possibilities.

It's guaranteed to be published in newspapers,
where headlines are capitalized
and your words are permanently printed in bold,
where your pictures
are publicly spread across the front pages
of what grand-daddy reads
and what grand-momma feeds
into the innermost parts of her soul.

Be choiceful as you evolve,
Dear Younger Me.

Your evolution will spark a revolution
that ignites a war
to disrupt your status quo
and interrupt the flow,
of societal conformities.
Shine a spotlight on your abnormalities
and highlight the tragedies
that will bookmark your life.

I've seen you get stuck in the quick sands
of shoulda, woulda and coulda beens.
So, let's bubble up atop the surface
to make yourself weightless,

by shedding anxiety and fear.
Step a few steps back
to power the pause that is right here.
Keep your hands free,
so that you may see
the branch that has been extended to me.
It will save your life.
Believe me when I tell you
that there is more within you,
my Dear Younger Me.

I am proud of you.

I remember when you thought like a child,
your mind moved with no consequence and no fear -
no fear in this world.
You were young, not dumb,
but full of some of the magic
that simply makes you, you.
But as you grew more seasoned,
I peppered you with insight,
sprinkled you with foresight,
and moved mountains
so you did not have to fight
this war on your own.

You will evolve with a strong army by your side,
to march you forward,
and upward,
and under,
and over.

This continuous change reminds us
that forward means nothing

when ascension is an option.
You are allergic to average.
So, rise, Dear Younger Me.

When you do what you've always done,
you'll get what you've always gotten,
so please know that you will be stuck at times,
in the warp of a matrix at times,
down on your luck at times,
but remember that God is always in those times.

The toxicity of people,
and processes,
and things,
help you know where you must not go,
but do you know where you are going?

You were born from generations of strength.
Will you choose to regress back from your future
or is your future back peddling from your past?
You were born absolute.
You are an Alpha in the making and
will roar until you become ready for the evolution!
For your evolution!

Your evolution will be televised.

Dust off the cobwebs of doubt
and stand up in the greatness
because you are who you are,
My Dear Younger Me.

Find the parallels to serve as footstools
that support your journey

on this obstacle-filled highway.
Invent tools to shatter ceilings
that seem impossible to attain,
break down doors
that were once locked
with deadbolts and chains.
Be that progression,
for you are the evolution
of my Dear Younger Me.

Dear Younger Me,
Can we talk?

This is to you, from me.
I love you,

Lolita

THE ENDING

As I penned each of these letters and poems, I imagined this book acting as a keepsake and go-to-reference to sit atop your coffee table, night stand, office desk, or serve as your favorite downloadable guide, reminding you that you are not alone in whatever you are feeling. I imagined you closing your eyes and allowing the message of your choosing to penetrate your soul. I imagined you grabbing hold of the content, then gifting yourself permission for my letters and poems to become art that helped reflect, reframe, and renew you. I imagined moments in my own life, where adding one of these letters and poems to my daily and weekly meditation would help me to drive an increased awareness and intention for my day.

I imagined the power of my words and colorful imagery within, as the light that impacts a nation - our nation, one journey at a time. As I read through the forty-four letters and poems in their entirety, I experienced a roller coaster ride of joy, frustration, tears, excitement, smiles and heartache. I recalled memories that I didn't realize were tucked away and emotions that I didn't know existed. I experienced a sense of being free, releasing baggage I didn't realize I was carrying and taking solace in knowing that there were others around the world who would hold these words sacred, as a healing space of comfort in their right now and a step toward progression on their paths forward. I remember asking God over and over again, to simply allow my words to flow authentically and clearly, such that they may be received by those who would benefit.

Whether for inspiration, motivation, or reassessment, I pray that I was able to meet you where you are, sans judgement, grab the innermost parts of you, and help you shift beyond today.

Thank you for trusting me on your journey.

Lolita

BEHIND THE BOOK

Can we talk?

A short dialogue between my maternal grandmother and I, a bit over a year ago, got this book rolling.

> *Lolita, sometimes I want to listen to something you've said but I don't know where or how to find it. Why not just print it and put it in a book for me to read?*

> *Well, Grandma Bea, this makes sense. I will put it in a book for you to read during the 91st year of life.*

For nearly one year, I was a bit lost when it came to the flow of this book. If you read my first book, *"The Intersection of You & Change,"* I gifted you short, relatable stories, affirmations through short poetry, then offered self-paced "soul work," as exercises and sacred spaces to craft your own stories, your own journey, to the unknown that awaited you.

My goal was to publish this second book a year later. God has a funny way of laughing at your plans. What I originally intended as a collection of stories, each concluding with a personalized affirmation, no longer served as a passion I felt led to bring to life. It wasn't because it no longer added value to the world, but more because it no longer lit the spark that felt most important to share with each of you at this time. The words I had written no longer shook me with the jolt of power and inspiration that I wanted and I needed for this published work. As my maternal grandmother sat at my parent's home in Accokeek, Maryland, feet resting upward in a recliner. It was in that very moment I suddenly became motivated. Now, if Grandma Bea was finding inspiration in my podcast, talks and appearances, why couldn't I simply ask she and others, can we talk?

2020 was a year to remember, some of which are within this book. 2021 marked the launch of my podcast, *Coaching, Cocktails, & Conversations,* and expanded my offerings under the same name. It also named my group coaching experience and stood out as curated forums on multiple voice and video social applications, yet, there was still a bubble of emptiness I was longing to investigate more deeply.

There was an imposter within me who questioned if my work was being heard and felt, despite the positive feedback that I was being given. This, singular chat with Grandma Bea, was a reminder that despite the season of life, we each have or will experience a shakiness in our confidence, a hindrance of self-doubt, devaluation of our worth, and fear of our unknown.

Grandma Bea, at 90, was not immune. I, at 44, am not immune. And regardless of age, we are not immune. Gender nor age will excuse us from these natural feelings and emotions.

This book captures the inner reflections that some of us may divulge aloud, some may keep to ourselves, some may use as guidance for others and some may simply want to forget all together. It is a collection of personal, professional, powerful, and sometimes poetic messages that will help us feel, what I refer to, as the *"power in our pause."* What if this "pause" possessed the power to cut ties with all that may be holding us back, at this very moment?

I thank you for allowing me to be, even a small part, of your journey.

Can we talk?

This is to you, from me.

255

I love you,

Lolita

THE AUTHOR

Lolita E. Walker is a sought-after, thought-leader, certified life coach and keynote speaker at the forefront of a movement that empowers busy women and high-powered organizations to feel and trust the power in their pause, reduce overwhelm, and move distractions to achieve un-deniable results, NOW. After leading in the corporate space for nearly twenty years, Lolita founded her personal and professional coaching and consultancy, Walker & Walker Enterprises – https://www.lolitawalker.com

A mommy of one son, Lolita's superpower is that she up-levels you through "spoken word gospel" to your mental, with the uncanny ability to pull the leadership and greatness that is hidden within. She is a certified life & executive coach, TEDx speaker, author of The Intersection of You & Change, podcast host of Coaching, Cocktails & Conversations, a retreat cultivator, and change champion for YOU. Courses, 1:1 and group coaching, personalized affirmations, and positive products, are only some of the complements to her public speaking and coaching practice.

Lolita graduated from Morgan State University as an Industrial Engineer and Simmons College as a Masters in Business Administration. She is a woman and minority-owned small business owner, an active member of Alpha Kappa Alpha Sorority, Incorporated and holds leadership positions in several organizations. She's been where you are and has gotten where you seek to be, in a renewed state of being. The benefit of having a partner who has reached the finish line successfully and systematically, is knowing that her methodologies are the enablers to help you and your teams soar beyond where they stand today.

Can we talk? https://www.lolitawalker.com.

THE ACKNOWLEDGEMENTS

To my Heavenly Father and the Lord of my life, *Jesus Christ*. My strength, my encouragement, my light when darkness threatens to cloud my mind and my compass when I lose my way on my path forward. Your presence, direction, and unconditional love are deeply and humbly appreciated and revered. Thank you.

To my son, *Walker*, who, at the age of 9, offers me a daily dose of joy, frustration, and amazement. You remain the epitome of strength, encouragement, energy, love, & living fearlessly free. You push me beyond my boundaries with the simplest of questions and then tap into a youth that I sometimes forget also resides within me. To my mommy, *Evelyn*, who has a renewed lens on life, supports each of my projects and passions and holds me up in ways that only a mother can. You are a much-appreciated footstool on my entrepreneurial journey, an arm and shoulder (literally) when I stumble and fall, and a resilient guide on my motherhood trek. I pray for increased love, happiness, and fulfillment all the days of your life. Thank you for always showing up. To my brother, *James-Douglas (JD)*, a calming voice through miles of separation, a positive reasoning in any situation and an encouraging motivator. You are a stronghold of unwavering faith. I am blessed to have been paired with you for my sibling love. I am so very proud of you for so many reasons. Thank you for simply being you. To my many aunts and uncles, in particular *Aunt Hope* and *Aunt Joy*, who through their Jamaican roots, carry on what my daddy would if he were still physically here. You listen to the drafts of each speech I write, help me celebrate my wins, feed me even when I am not hungry and provide wisdom I may not ask for, yet definitely need; my DC and Virginia family, in particular my cousins, *Ronnie, Byron, Elmora, Joy* and *Alice*, who provide a safe haven for Walker, my mini me, and a get-away for "mommy-moments" when I need. You double as the chairpersons of every aspect of my business. Thank you. My best friend *Faye*, who is one of the strongest and most focused human beings I know and the creator of this book's title. Thank you for being you. Your creativity is out of this world and your love and support is unmatched. Thank you for knowing when it's the right time to jump in; it's always when I need you the most. Regardless of time, distance, or circumstance, our bond remains as vibrant as the day that we met.

Damon Jones, the author of the forward within this book and a pure vessel of drive, deliberateness, and excellence. You have instilled in me leadership and intention, as I climbed the corporate ladder. You are the communications expert who helped to strengthen my toolkit of digging deeper into the "why" of any conversation, then leaving space for the uncomfortable "pause." **Danne Smith Mathis, Stacy Luckett and Ramon Ray,** who selflessly pre-read this manuscript with open eyes and a willingness of honestly in its power. I thank you for saying yes to an authentic connection made through an audio application. I do not take for granted your time, energy and friendship. Thank you. *Carla*, my line sister of the Alpha Delta Chapter of Alpha Kappa Alpha Sorority, Incorporated, who simultaneously acts as a mother and a sister, asking the hard questions that no one else dares. Thank you for journeying with me through my tears, laughs, and growth; *Qiana, Safiyyah*, and **Lavonda**, my "divas" and individual sounding boards, who hold me up, down and all the way around. You have comforted me at my lowest and held me at my highest. You have supported me when I felt there was no way I could move forward and you have pushed me to leap, even when I forgot that my faith and strengths had wings. You gave me the strength I needed to fall. Your genuine care for me is deep and I do not take that for granted. Thank you. I struggle to put into words what each of you mean to me, so I simply say thank you for being you. **Tarik Sankofa**, you helped me rediscover the poetic depths of me. Your talent is indescribable and I am so blessed to have met you on my path to reclaim the "bolder" me. The magic of art that surround your words are genius.

I thank you for pushing me even when I didn't recognize that I was the greatness that others had yet to see.

Finally, to my father, **Emanuel A. Walker**, my heartbeat that no longer beats, yet still challenges me daily. You are, by far, my biggest cheerleader, on and beyond this earth. May you forever be proud at the energy I put into this world. May you smile ear to ear, knowing the lessons you instilled in me continue to nourish those listed above. May you also smile with your mom, **Grandma Lucille Walker,** who, at 91 years-young, joined you in a heavenly peace, where I know God simply said, "my child, well-done."

A reminder to each of you reading and listening, particularly **my clients and customers** who have trusted me on your individual and collective journeys; I love and appreciate you and would not be here without you. Your support, encouragement, prayers, and love mean the world to me. Thank you.

My company stands on the foundation of the two strongest pillars of change in my life - my father, last name Walker and son, first name Walker. I stand at the forefront of our enterprise.

WALKER & WALKER
E N T E R P R I S E S

....

www.lolitawalker.com

THE BONUS

I.   Soul Work

If you have read my first book, *The Intersection of You & Change,* followed me on any social platform, leveraged me for keynote speaking or workshops, been a client of any of my coaching services, you know that I love gifting soul work to empower you to reflectively challenge your thinking. Here's the soul work curated just for you.

- Which letter or poem did you resonate with the most?

  _____

- How many times did you listen to words of this poem?

  _____

- What about it helped you to pause?

  _____

  _____

  _____

- What emotion did it evoke from you?

  _____

- What memories, if any, did it rise for you?

  _____

  _____

  _____

- What three things will you sit with for reflection and/or action, as a result of the poem?

  _____

  _____

  _____

II.   A Poem to My Grandma Lucille

We have each experienced loss.
As I wrote these letters and poems, my 91 years young, paternal grandmother, passed away. In memory of my Grandma Lucille Walker, here is an excerpt of the piece that I wrote and read at her homegoing services. For her family and loved ones, may it be a forever reminder of her life on this earth.

....

Dear Grandma Lucille,
91 years,
nine decades plus one,
you were blessed with the sun
to shine on your heavenly being.
We thank God for you.

You served as a lent child upon this earth.
You gave birth to souls of daughters and sons,
of grands and great-grands.

You left footprints in the sand
of love,
of legacy,
of bits of Lucille Walker that will forever be within me.
I want to say thank you.

Had I known it would be our last time together,
I would have hugged you just a little bit tighter
and not taken for granted
that our together, would be forever.
I want to say thank you.

It is in your stillness,
where we can forever say
that we've gathered in memory
of your yesteryears,
with images of forever's that are closing near.
I want to say thank you.

Our souls remain interlocked.
Your spirit penetrates this place
in this moment, in this time.
I want to say thank you.

As the deepness of your dimples
illuminate your contagious smile
and all the while,
their depth cradles us with hugs and with love,
we remember the strength that came from our father above.

I want to say thank you, Heavenly Father
for granting us the space.
I want to say thank you, Heavenly Father
for allowing her in these places,
where she has touched so many.
I want to say thank you, Grandma Lucille.

We sing your forever spiritual love,
"It is well, it is well, with my soul."

Your tenacity breathes life into my being.
Your strength strings wisdom into my essence.
Your gifts lend a piece into my vision.
I want to say thank you.

So Dear Grandma Lucille,

I long for the day that I see you again.

Until then,
I have thoughts and fond memories
that won't ever go away.
You will always give way
to some of the best pieces of who I am today.

Dear Grandma Lucille,
This is to you, from me.

I love you.
Your granddaughter,

Lolita

Notes & Reflections

Notes & Reflections

Can We Talk?

Letters & Poems to Reclaim a Bolder You

WALKER & WALKER
E N T E R P R I S E S

....

www.lolitawalker.com

2022